Failure to Quit

FAILURE TO QUIT

Reflections of an Optimistic Historian

_____

Howard Zinn

South End Press

CAMBRIDGE, MASSACHUSETTS

"Perils of Plato," "'Je Ne Suis Pas un Marxiste'" (originally published as "Nothing Human is Alien to Me"), "Objections to Objectivity," "The Optimism of Uncertainty," and "Failure to Quit" have appeared in *Z Magazine;* "The Supreme Court is Not Supreme" appeared in *Civil Liberties Review;* "The Problem is Civil Obedience" appeared in *Violence: The Crisis of American Confidence* (Johns Hopkins Press, 1972); "How Free is Higher Education?" appeared in the *Gannett Center Journal;* "Columbus, the Indians, and Human Progress" appeared as an Open Magazine pamphlet.

Cover design by Kyle G. Hunter
Front cover photograph (taken at a demonstration in Boston) by Lee
Lockwood
Back cover photograph by Jeff Zinn

Library of Congress Cataloging-in-Publication Data

Zinn, Howard, 1922–
    Failure to quit : reflections of an optimistic historian / Howard Zinn.
        p. cm. — (The radical 60s ; v. 7)
    Originally published: Monroe, Me. : Common Courage Press, 1993.
    ISBN 0-89608-676-3 (pbk. : alk. paper)
        1. Zinn, Howard, 1922– — Political and social views. 2. United
    States—Historiography. 3. United States—History—Philosophy
    4. United States—Politics and government—Philosophy. 5. Human
    rights—Philosophy. I. Title. II. Radical 60s ; v. 7.

E175.5.Z56 A25 2002
973'.07'2—dc21
                                                            2002029157

South End Press
7 Bookline Street, #1
Cambridge, MA 02139-4146
www.southendpress.org

06 05 04 03 02   1 2 3 4 5

To Staughton and Alice Lynd,
who refuse to quit.

Contents

Preface to the South End Press Edition

In 1986, President Ronald Reagan, in his continuing efforts—both legal and illegal—to overthrow the revolutionary Sandinista government in Nicaragua, declared a blockade of that small Central American country. Tens of thousands of Americans had signed a Pledge of Resistance to commit civil disobedience if warlike measures were undertaken against the Sandinistas. In Boston, five hundred and fifty people, I among them, occupied the federal building downtown, and refused to leave. We were all arrested, held for a while, then released. It proved too big a job, perhaps too embarrassing an undertaking, to prosecute so many, and the charges were dropped. I received notice of that, and for the first time learned what we were all being charged with: "Failure to quit the premises"—an old Massachusetts statute to deal with trespassing. I thought that phrase "failure to quit" perfectly epitomized the determination of people all over the country to protest government actions they saw as violations of human rights, whether here or abroad. So when Common Courage Press put together a group of my essays on various subjects, we decided to call the book *Failure to Quit*.

Introduction

Introducing a bunch of writings (the word anthology, originally meaning a collection of flowers, would be going too far) requires a certain amount of ingenuity, finding a common thread in pieces that were written at different times, in response to different situations.

The difficulty is compounded in this case, where some of the pieces are transcripts of talks: ranging from a Vietnam-era debate at Johns Hopkins University to more recent lectures at the University of Wisconsin and the University of Minnesota, a talk for the Civil Liberties Union of Massachusetts, and a lecture at the Wellfleet Public Library broadcast on WOMR, Cape Cod, organized by those super-organizers, Robert and Ethel Levy.

Others are essays, written for the now-defunct (am I responsible?) *Civil Liberties Review,* or the (also defunct; my record is getting worse by the minute) *Gannett Center Journal.* Five of the shorter pieces were written for *Z Magazine.* One was written for the Open Magazine Pamphlet Series.

One entry is an unpublished Op-Ed piece. And one is an interview with the extraordinary radio persona David Barsamian.

The closest I can come to finding a common thread is that all the pieces represent the thinking of someone who wants to address urgent issues of peace and justice with the perspective (presumably long-range and very wise) of a historian.

The stimulus for putting these together came from Greg Bates, who claims to run Common Courage Press from someplace in Maine, but I have never laid eyes on him or his locus of operations in Maine, so I am only assuming they exist. All I can say is that he is very engaging on the telephone, good-humored, easy to work with. Add those qualities to invisibility and you have the perfect editor-publisher.

The question now is whether we have matched such a publisher with a proper writer. I leave that judgment to the reader.

Howard Zinn
March 1993

"Who Controls the Past Controls the Future"

Interview with David Barsamian

This interview took place in Boulder, Colorado in 1992, and David Barsamian and I had a lot of fun with it, which is hard to recapture in a transcript, so readers will have to content themselves with what is left after the tape was scrupulously edited to remove the fun. I met David some years ago when I was invited to speak in Boulder by a remarkable veteran journalist named Sender Garlin, now ninety and brimming with energy. David has been a pioneer in what is mysteriously called "alternative radio," and when I spoke a few years ago to a national conference of several hundred "alternative radio" people, everyone seemed to know him. He drew from me things about my life which I was saving for my own slightly shorter version of *Remembrance of Things Past*.

1992

Barsamian: *I want to know something about your roots, growing up in the projects on the lower East Side.*

I grew up in the slums of Brooklyn. Not projects. They weren't advanced enough to have projects. I think maybe the first New Deal housing project was in Williamsburg, Brooklyn. But that was too good for us. I grew up in the slums of Brooklyn, a working class family. My parents were European immigrants, factory workers in New York. They met as factory workers. They were Jewish immigrants. My father came from Austria, my mother from Asiatic Russia, Siberia. I remember moving all the time. We were always one step ahead of the landlord. And changing schools all the time. My father struggled, went from job to job, he was unemployed and under WPA. I wanted to get out of the

3

house all the time. Where we lived was never a nice place to be. So I was in the streets a lot. I understand what it's like for kids to live in and prefer the streets. That's how I grew up. When I got to be college age I went to work in a shipyard and became a shipyard worker for three years. My family needed the money. The East Side came later, after the war. I volunteered for the Air Force and was a bombardier. I got married before I went overseas. After the war my wife and I first lived in Bedford-Stuyvesant in a rat-infested basement. I'm building up my sordid past, trying to evoke tears. We were so happy when we were accepted into the Lillian Wald housing project, a low-income housing project on the East Side of New York. We lived there for seven years while I went to New York University under the GI Bill and to graduate school at Columbia. My wife worked. Our two kids were in nursery school.

Barsamian: *What was the language at home? Did you speak Yiddish?*

Not me. My parents spoke Yiddish to each other, so I understood it. When they spoke to us they spoke English, nicely accented, with a few Yiddish words thrown in. I never actually used Yiddish, but I still can understand it. Words like "bagel" and "knish."

Barsamian: *I remember you telling me about your father being a waiter for many years. He'd work a bar mitzvah and then there'd be no work, and then he'd do a bat mitzvah.*

He did a lot of Jewish weddings. In fact, when I was about seventeen he introduced me to it. On New Year's Eve they would be short and the waiters would be able to bring their sons in. They called them "juniors." It was an AFL craft union. Everything was hereditary: the leadership of the union, the jobs, etc. I really hated being a waiter, and I felt for my father. They used to call him "Charlie Chaplin" because he walked like Charlie Chaplin. His feet were flat. They said it was the result of all those years of being a waiter. I don't know if that's true or not, but that was the story. He worked very hard. He was a great fan of Roosevelt during the New Deal, he and a lot of other people who didn't have any jobs any more. People were still getting married, but they weren't paying waiters, so my father worked as a ditch digger with the WPA. My mother had been a factory worker before she was married. When she got married she began having kids, and it was my father's job to support the family.

Barsamian: *Was there any kind of intellectual life at home, books, magazines?*

No. There were no books or magazines. The very first book I read I picked up on the street. Ten pages were ripped off, but it didn't matter to me because it was my first book. I was already reading, and this was *Tarzan and the Jewels of Opar*. I'll always remember that. No books at home. However, my parents knew that I liked books and liked to read. The *New York Post* came out with this gift, that if you clipped these coupons and sent in twenty-five cents, they would send you a volume of Dickens. So my parents sent away for the whole set of Dickens, the collected works, twenty volumes. I read every single one. Dickens was my first author. Some of them I didn't understand, like *The Pickwick Papers*. Sometimes I got the humor and sometimes I didn't. I went through them in order. I thought if the *New York Post* sent you the books in order, somehow they must have a reason for it. So first it was *David Copperfield*, then *Oliver Twist*, then *Dombey and Son*, then *Bleak House*.

When I was thirteen my parents bought me a typewriter. They didn't know about typewriters or books, but they knew I was interested in reading and writing, so they paid five dollars for a remade Underwood No. 5, which I had for a very long time.

Barsamian: *I want you to talk about your World War Two bombardier experience. I've heard you discuss it in public lectures, and you write about it. There were two missions in particular that you always mention, one over Pilsen in Czechoslovakia and the other in France in the town of Royan. Why are they so important to you?*

These things weren't important at the time. I was just another member of the Air Force doing my duty, listening to my briefings before going out on the flight and dropping the bombs where I was supposed to, without thinking, where am I dropping them? What am I doing? Who lives here? What's going on here? I flew the last missions of the war. By then we were well into Germany. We were running out of targets, and so we were bombing Eastern Europe. I dropped bombs on Hungary. I remember the raid on Pilsen. A lot of planes went over. I remember reading about the raid after the war. It was described by Churchill in his memoirs as, Well, we bombed Pilsen and there were very few civilian casualties. Then I was in Europe years after that, sometime in the mid-1960s, in Yugoslavia. I ran into a couple from Pilsen. Hesitantly, I told them that I had been in one of the crews that bombed Pilsen. They said, when you finished the streets were full of corpses, hundreds and hundreds of people killed in that raid.

It was only after the war that I began to think about the raids I had been on. The thing about being in the Air Force and dropping bombs from 35,000 feet is that you don't see anybody, human beings, you don't hear screams, see blood, see mangled bodies. I understand very well how atrocities are committed in modern warfare: from a distance. So there I was doing these things.

The raid on Royan was an even more difficult experience for me as I thought about it later. It was just a few months before the end of the war. We thought we weren't going to fly any more missions, because we had already overrun France, taken most of Germany, there was virtually nothing left to bomb, and everybody knew the war was going to be over in a few weeks. We were awakened at one in the morning, the usual waking up time if you're going to fly at six. It's not like in the movies where you leap out of bed into the cockpit, rev up the engines and you're off. Five boring hours of listening to briefings, getting your equipment, putting on your electrically heated suit, going to the bombardiers' briefing, the officers' briefing, going to eat and deciding whether you eat square eggs or round eggs. That means powdered eggs or real eggs. If you were going on a bombing mission you got real eggs—as many as you wanted. They briefed us and told us we were going to bomb this little town on the Atlantic coast near Bordeaux, a town called Royan. They showed it to us on the map. Nobody asked why. You don't ask questions at briefings. To this day I feel ashamed that it didn't even occur to me to ask, Why are we doing this when the war is almost over? Why are we bombing this little French town when France is all ours? There were a few thousand German soldiers holed up near this town, waiting for the war to end, not doing anything, not bothering anybody. But we were going to destroy them.

So twelve hundred heavy bombers were sent over. I didn't know how many bombers were sent. All I knew was my squadron of twelve bombers were going over. I could see other squadrons. It wasn't until later, when I did research into it after the war, that I realized that it was twelve hundred heavy bombers going over against two or three thousand German soldiers. But they told us in the briefing, You're going to carry a different type of bomb in the bomb bay. Not the usual demolition bomb. You're going to carry canisters, long cylinders of jellied gasoline. It didn't mean anything to us, except we knew jellied gasoline would ignite. It was napalm.

It was only after the war that I began to think about that raid and did some research and visited Royan. I went into the ruins of the library, now rebuilt, and read what they had written about it. I wrote an essay about that bombing. It epitomized the stupidity of modern warfare and how the momentum of military machines carries armies on to do the most atrocious things that any rational person sitting down for five minutes and thinking about it would stop immediately.

So we destroyed the town, the German soldiers, the French also who were there. In one of my essays I coupled it with the bombing of Hiroshima as two bombings that at the time, I am ashamed to say, I welcomed. With Royan it wasn't that I welcomed it, I was just doing it. With Hiroshima I welcomed it because it meant that the war would end and I wouldn't have to go to the Pacific and fly any more bombing missions.

Barsamian: *Some years after that, in the mid-1960s, you visited Hiroshima. You had intended to make certain remarks at a gathering of survivors. You weren't able to make those remarks.*

It was a terrible moment. A few Americans were visiting Hiroshima every August, an international gathering to commemorate the dropping of the bomb. We were taken to visit a house of survivors, where people who had survived Hiroshima gathered and socialized with one another. They brought this little international group, a few Americans, a Frenchman, a Russian. The Japanese, the survivors, were sitting on the floor. We were expected to get up and say something to them as visitors from other countries. The Russian woman spoke about what the Russians had suffered in the war and how she could commiserate with the Japanese. As I planned to get up and speak, I thought, I don't know what I can say. But I have to be honest. I have to say I was a bombardier, even though I didn't bomb Japan. I bombed people, innocent people, civilians, just as in Hiroshima. So I got up to speak and looked out at the people sitting there. Suddenly something happened to my eyesight, my brain. I saw this blur of people who were blind, with missing arms, missing legs, people whose skin was covered with sores. This was real. That's what these people looked like. I looked out at them and I couldn't speak. In all the speaking I've ever done, nothing like that has ever happened to me. It was impossible. I just stood there. My voice choked up. That was it.

Barsamian: *I'd like to focus now on something else. What about the notion of history as a commodity, something that can be bought and sold. Do you accept that?*

I once wrote an essay called "History as Private Enterprise." What I meant was that I thought so much history was written without a social conscience behind it. Or if there was a social conscience somewhere in the historian, it was put aside for the writing of history, because writing history was done as a professional duty. It was done to get something published, to get a job at a university, to get tenure, to get a promotion, to build up one's prestige. It was printed by publishers in books that would sell and make a profit. The profit motive, which has so distorted our whole economic and social system by making profit the key to what is produced and therefore leaving important things unproduced and stupid things produced and leaving some people rich and some people poor. That same profit system had extended to that world, which as an innocent young student I thought was a world separated from the world of commerce and business. But the world of the university, of publishing, of history, of scholarship is not at all separated from the profit-seeking world. The historian doesn't think of it consciously this way. But there is the fact of economic security that operates in every profession. The professional writer and historian is perhaps conscious, perhaps semiconscious, or perhaps it has already been absorbed into the bloodstream, is thinking about economic security and therefore about playing it safe. So we get a lot of safe history.

Barsamian: *You're fond of quoting Orwell's dictum*

"Who controls the past controls the future. Who controls the present controls the past."

Orwell is one of my favorite writers in general. When I came across that I knew I had to use it. We writers are real thieves. We see something good and use it, and then if we're nice we say where we got it. Sometimes we don't. What the Orwell quote means to me is a very important observation that if you can control history, what people know about history, if you can decide what's in people's history and what's left out, you can order their thinking. You can order their values. You can in effect organize their brains by controlling their knowledge. The people who can do that, who can control the past, are the people who control the present. The people who would dominate the media, who publish the textbooks, who decide in our culture what are the dominant ideas, what gets told and what doesn't.

Barsamian: *Who are they? Who are the guardians of the past? Can you make some general comments about their class background, race?*

They are mostly guys, mostly well off, mostly white. Sometimes this is talked about as the history of rich, white men. There's a history which is done by rich white men. Not that historians are rich. But the people who publish the textbooks are, the people who control the media, the people who decide what historians to invite on the networks at special moments when they want to call on a historian. The people who dominate the big media networks, they're rich. Not only are the controllers of our information rich and white and male, but they then ask that history concentrate on those who are rich and white and male. That is why the point of view of black people has not been a very important one in the telling of our history. The point of view of women certainly has not been. The point of view of working people is something that has not been given its due in the histories that we have mostly been given in our culture.

Barsamian: *You've made the astounding comment that objectivity and scholarship in the media and elsewhere is not only "harmful and misleading, it's not desirable."*

I've said two things about it. One, that it's not possible. Two, it's not desirable. It's not possible because all history is a selection out of an infinite number of facts. As soon as you begin to select, you select according to what you think is important. Therefore it is already not objective. It's already biased in the direction of whatever you, as the selector of this information, think people should know. So it's really not possible.

Some people claim to be objective. The worst thing is to claim to be objective. Of course you can't be. Historians should say what their values are, what they care about, what their background is, and let you know what is important to them so that young people and everybody who reads history are warned in advance that they should never count on any one source, but should go to many sources. So it's not possible to be objective, and it's not desirable if it were possible. We should have history that does reflect points of view and values, in other words, history that is not objective. We should have history that enhances human values, humane values, values of brotherhood, sisterhood, peace, justice, and equality. The closest I can get to it is the values enunciated in the Declaration of Independence. Equality, the right of all people to have life, liberty, and the pursuit of happiness. Those are values that historians should actively promulgate in writing history. In doing that they needn't distort or omit important things. But it does mean if they have those values in mind, that they will emphasize those things in history which will bring up a new generation of people who read history books and who will care about treating other people equally, about doing away with war, about justice in every form.

Barsamian: *How do you filter those biases, or can*

you even filter them?

As I've said, yes, I have my biases, my leanings. So if I'm writing or speaking about Columbus, I will try not to hide or omit the fact that Columbus did a remarkable thing in crossing the ocean and venturing out into uncharted waters. It took physical courage and navigational skill. It was a remarkable event. I have to say that so that I don't omit what people see as the positive side of Columbus. But then I have to go on to say the other things about Columbus which are much more important than his navigational skill, than the fact that he was a religious man. His treatment of the human beings that he found in this hemisphere. The enslavement, the torture, the murder, the dehumanization of these people. That is the important thing.

There's an interesting way in which you can frame a sentence which will show what you emphasize and which will have two very different results. Here's what I mean. Take Columbus as an example. You can frame it, and this was the way the Harvard historian Samuel Eliot Morison in effect framed it in his biography of Columbus: Columbus committed genocide, but he was a wonderful sailor. He did a remarkable and extraordinary thing in finding these islands in the Western Hemisphere. Where's the emphasis there? He committed genocide, but...he's a good sailor. I say, He was a good sailor, but he treated people with the most horrible cruelty and committed genocide. Those are two different ways of saying the same facts. Depending on which side of the "but" you're on, you show your bias. I believe that it's good for us to put our biases in the direction of a humane view of history.

Barsamian: *I know you were present at the 1892 celebration of the four-hundredth anniversary of Columbus's voyage...*

Of course, I try to be at all these important events. I tried to be there in 1492 but I didn't make it.

Barsamian: *In terms of 1992, were you surprised at the level of protest, indignation, and general criticism of Columbus?*

I was delightfully surprised. I did expect more protest this year than there ever has been, because I knew, just from going around the country speaking and from reactions to my book [*A People's History of the United States*], which has sold a couple of hundred thousand copies. It starts off with Columbus, so anybody who has read my book is going to have a different view of Columbus, I hope. I knew that there had been more literature in the last few years. Hans Koning's wonderful book, which appeared before mine, *Columbus: His Enterprise*, to give one example. I was aware that Native American groups around the country were planning protests. So I knew that things would happen, but I really wasn't prepared for the number of things that have happened and the extent of protest that there has been. It has been very satisfying. What's interesting about it, much as people like me and you rail against the media, they don't have total control. It is possible for us, and this is a very heartwarming thing and it should be encouraging, even though we don't control the major media and major publishing organizations, by sheer word of mouth, a little radio broadcast, community newspapers, speaking here and there, Noam Chomsky speaking seventeen times a day in a hundred cities, it's possible by doing these things to actually change the culture in a very important way. When the *New York Times* had a story saying that this year the Columbus quincentennial is marked by protests, it became clear that the challenge was noticed. In Denver they called off a parade because of the protest that they expected. This has happened in a number of other places. Berkeley changed Columbus Day to Indigenous Peoples Day.

Barsamian: *So in this doom and gloom atmosphere that the left loves to wash itself in at times there are glimpses of light?*

Traveling around the country I am encouraged by
what I see. Not just about Columbus, but that as soon as you
give people information that they didn't have before, they
are ready to accept it. When I went around the country
speaking about Columbus, I was worried that suddenly, as
I started telling about these atrocities that Columbus committed, people in the audience would start yelling and
shouting and throwing things at me, threatening my life.
That hasn't happened at all. Maybe the worst that happened is that one Italian-American said to me in a low
voice, plaintively, "What are Italians going to do? Who are
we going to celebrate?" I said, "Joe DiMaggio, Arturo Tos-
canini, Pavarotti, Fiorello LaGuardia, a whole bunch of
wonderful Italians that we can celebrate."

It's been very encouraging. I believe that all over this
country there are people who really want change. I don't
mean the miniscule change that Clinton represents. I suppose a miniscule change is better than no change that we've
been having. But there are people around this country who
want much more change than the parties are offering.

Barsamian: *Are you encouraged also by the devel-
opment of new media, community radio stations, cable TV,
Z, Common Courage Press, South End Press and the Open
Magazine pamphlet series?*

Oh, yes.

Barsamian: *Is there anything in American history
that parallels this burst of independent media in the last
ten or fifteen years?*

There have been periods in American history when
pamphlets and newspapers have had an important effect in
arousing and organizing a movement. In the period leading
up to the Revolutionary War there was a lot of pamphle-
teering that was not under the control of the colonial governors. In the time of the antislavery movement, the

abolitionists, the antislavery people spread literature all over the country. So much so that Andrew Jackson ordered the Postmaster General to bar abolitionist literature from the Southern states. That's Andrew Jackson, our great hero. We've had labor newspapers, the populist movement put out an enormous number of pamphlets.

But in this era of television and radio, where they soon became dominated by these monstrous, fabulously wealthy networks crowding critical voices off the air, it's been very refreshing just in the past few years to see these new media. I could see this in the Gulf War. I was invited to a gathering of several hundred community broadcasters in Boston. I didn't know so many existed. During the Gulf War they were about the only place where you could hear critical voices, Noam Chomsky and other people who would give you an analysis of the war in a critical way. You weren't getting that on public television, certainly not on the major media. Now there are satellite dishes. It's amazing that people in the progressive movement are able to use these satellite dishes to beam broadcasts all over. Wherever I go there are community newspapers. That's what we have to depend on, and we should make the most of it.

Barsamian: *In the popular culture, ideology and propaganda are attributes of our adversaries. It's not something that we have here in our democracy. How do you persuade people in your talks and writings that in fact there is a good deal of propaganda and a great amount of ideology right here in the United States?*

The best way I can persuade them that what we get mostly from the media and the textbooks and the histories is ideological, biased not in the humanist direction but towards wealth and power, expansion, militarism, and conquest, is to give them examples from history and to show how the government has manipulated our information. You can go back to the Spanish-American War and talk about how the history textbooks all said that the reason we got into that war was that popular opinion demanded it. Therefore the president went along. There were no public opinion polls then, no mass rallies on behalf of going into Cuba. By public opinion they meant a few powerful newspapers. So when I get to the Vietnam War I talk about how the government manipulated the information, not only the general public, but the newspapers, Congress, how they fabricated incidents in the Gulf of Tonkin in the summer of 1964 to give Lyndon Johnson an excuse to go before Congress and get them to pass a resolution giving him carte blanche to start the war full-scale. I talk about the history books and how they omit what the United States has done in Latin America, and how when they get to the Spanish-American War they will talk about what we did in Cuba but not much about what we did in the Philippines. The war in Cuba lasted three months, while the war in the Philippines lasted for years. A big, bloody, Vietnam-type war. So I try to give historical examples to show how that ideology manifests itself.

Barsamian: *Speaking of the Vietnam War, it seems it never ends, never will end. You saw examples of that in the 1992 presidential campaign, about draft status, who fought and who didn't. And the ongoing MIA / POW issue. Why is that? Why does it persist?*

The administrations, the powers that be, the people who got us into the Vietnam War and kept us in it, didn't like the way it ended. They're trying to change the ending, to rewrite history. They're saying, the reason we lost is because of the media, the antiwar movement. Or we fought with one hand behind our back. We dropped seven million tons of bombs, twice as much as we dropped in World War II, and that was "one hand tied behind our back." Incredible. They were very unhappy not just that we lost the war, but that people became aware of what happened in the war, became aware of the carnage. The My Lai massacre. The destruction of the Vietnamese countryside. The deaths of a million people in Vietnam and of 55,000 Americans. They worry that those events made the American people leery of military intervention. All the surveys taken after the Vietnam War in the late 1970s showed that the American people did not want military intervention anywhere in the world, for any reason. The establishment has been trying desperately—the military-industrial-political establishment—to change that view and to try to get the American people to accept military intervention as once more the basic American policy. Grenada was a probe, Panama another, the war in the Middle East a bigger one.

Barsamian: *They were all short and fast.*

Exactly. They learned a number of things from Vietnam. If you're going to have a war, do it quickly. Don't give the public a chance to know what's happening. Control the information, so the war will be over before anybody really knows the truth about what happened. Here it is now, a year or two years later, and only now we're finding out that the Bush Administration was arming Saddam Hussein right up to just before the war. So keep the war short. And try to have very few casualties, and don't mention the casualties on the other side. Then you can call it a "costless war." Even if 100,000 Iraqis die, even if tens of thousands of children die in Iraq, they don't count as people. So you can say it was an easy war.

Barsamian: *You're fond also of quoting Chomsky and Edward Herman in* Manufacturing Consent. *They observe that it's hard to make a case about the manipulation of the media when they find that they're so willing to go along.*

I like that quote because so many people fall in with the media when the media say the government is controlling the information. They say, we want desperately to tell the truth to the public. But of course they don't. In the Iraqi war they showed themselves to be such weak, pathetic, absolutely obsequious yea-sayers to the briefers in Washington. They kept putting generals and ex-Joint Chiefs of Staff personnel on the air, military experts, to make us all exult in the smart bombs that were being dropped. The media did not use anybody who would give any historical background, or who would criticize the war on the air.

Barsamian: *One of your intellectual favorites is Alan Dershowitz. In a recent column he was writing about the atrocities in the Balkans and decrying the use of the Nazi analogy. He says it is "overused and automatically invoked and as a result nearly bereft of cognitive content." What do you think of that?*

Analogies have to be used carefully. They can be misused, and sometimes they are not used as analogies but as identities, and if you say something is like something, people will say, Oh, you're saying it *is* that. It is possible to overuse the Nazi analogy until it loses its force. I was speaking to a group of high school students in Boston the other day. One of them asked, Who was worse, Hitler or Columbus? There's a nice analogy. They are two different situations, two different forms of genocide. In fact, in that situation it was not an exaggeration. In terms of the numbers of people who died, the Hitler killing was smaller than the number of people who died in the genocide not committed directly by Columbus, but as a result of the work of the *conquistadores*, Columbus, and the others, when they got through with the Caribbean and Latin America. Perhaps fifty million people or more died, the indigenous population, as a result of enslavement, overwork, direct execution, disease, a much higher toll even than the genocide of Hitler.

I think it's all right to invoke analogies, so long as you invoke them carefully and make clear what the differences are and the similarities.

Barsamian: *In addition to wiping out the indige-*

nous population, the Europeans had to initiate the slave trade and bring over the Africans to work the land.

When the Indians were gone as workers, that's when the slave trade began, and another genocide took place, tens of millions of black slaves brought over, dying by the millions on the way and then dying in great numbers when they got here.

Barsamian: *In that same Dershowitz column, he talks about the uniqueness of the Jewish Holocaust in terms of genocide, that it stands by itself. Would you accept that?*

It depends on what you mean by "unique." Every genocide obviously stands by itself in that every genocide has its own peculiar historical characteristics. But I think it is wrong, and we should understand that, to take any one genocide and concentrate on it to the neglect of others and act as if there has only been one great genocide in the world and nobody should bring up any other because it's a poor analogy. The greatest gift the Jews could give to the world is not to remember Hitler's genocide for exactly what it was, that is, the genocide of Jews, but to take what that horrible experience was for Jews and then to apply it to all the other things that are going on in the world, where huge numbers of people are dying for no reason at all. Apply it to the starvation in Somalia and the way people are treated by the advanced industrial countries in the Third World, where huge numbers of people die in wars or for economic reasons. I think in that sense what happened in the Holocaust is not unique. It should not be left alone. It should be applied everywhere it can, because that is past. The other genocides are present and future.

Barsamian: *Let's talk a little about Hollywood and history. Michael Parenti, in a book entitled* Make-Believe Media, *suggests that in an increasingly non-literate soci-*

ety, film has the "last frame," the last chapter of history. I'd like you to connect that with a discussion about Oliver Stone's docudrama JFK. He has said, "The American people deserve to have their history back." What about the assumption that history was once ours and is now lost?

Of course, it was never ours. History has always belonged to the people who controlled whatever present there was. They control history. So it's not a matter of taking it back. Very often people will say, Let us restore America to what it once was. To what? Slavery? Let us restore the good old days? The good old days lie ahead. Film is tremendously important. I don't know whether it's the last frame. I'm even dubious about whether films, as powerful as they are at the moment that they capture you, have the lasting effect that literature and writing have. I don't know this for sure. We have fewer and fewer people reading books. Are the statistics on that clear? I know everybody says this. I know that students are not reading books the way they used to. I know there are millions of people in this country who read books, and obviously many more millions who don't read books. In that sense it's true. They are watching videos, watching television, and going to the movies. People who are not reached by books have only videos, movies, and television. Then they become especially important. I agree with the importance of the visual media. I love the movies. I'm very happy when I see a movie made that I think does something to advance people's social consciousness. I have a special place in my heart for movies that have something important to say.

When I saw Oliver Stone's movie *Salvador* I thought it was a very powerful statement about the brutal American policy supporting the dictatorship and the death squads of El Salvador. When I saw *Born on the Fourth of July*, I thought, This is great. He's bringing the antiwar movement before millions of people and showing that there's no conflict between soldiers in Vietnam and the antiwar movement. Soldiers came back from Vietnam and joined the antiwar movement, as Ron Kovic did.

When I saw *JFK* I did not have the same feeling. I thought he was contradicting what he was doing in *Born on the Fourth of July*, where he was saying, We had an antiwar movement in this country. If the war came to an end, it was in good part because people like Ron Kovic and Vietnam veterans and all the other people who protested against the war showed us what a social movement was like. But in *JFK* he is telling us that the key to ending the war was the president of the United States. If Kennedy had lived he would have ended the war. That viewpoint perpetuates an elitist notion in history which I've been struggling against. I think that Oliver Stone in his better films is also struggling against it, the idea that history is made from the top, and if we want change to come about we must depend on our presidents, on the Supreme Court, on Congress. If history shows anything, to me, it shows that we cannot depend on those people on top to make the necessary changes towards justice and peace. It's social movements we must depend on to do that.

The Optimism of Uncertainty

The word "optimism," used here, and in the subtitle of my book, makes me a little uneasy, because it suggests a blithe, slightly sappy whistler in the dark of our time. But I use it anyway, not because I am totally confident that the world will get better, but because I am certain that *only* such confidence can prevent people from giving up the game before all the cards have been played. The metaphor is deliberate; it is a gamble. Not to play is to foreclose any chance of winning. To play, to *act*, is to create at least a possibility of changing the world. I wrote this essay to show that there is some evidence in support of that possibility. I should mention that I first wrote about this in a much longer piece requested by John Tirman of the Winston Foundation.

1988

As this century draws to a close, a century packed with history, what leaps out from that history is its utter unpredictability.

This confounds us, because we are talking about exactly the period when human beings became so ingenious technologically that they could plan and predict the exact time of someone landing on the moon.

But who foresaw that, 24 years after the national Democratic Party Convention refused to seat blacks from Mississippi, a black militant would run for president, excite crowds, black and white, all over the country, and then dominate the Democratic Party Convention in Atlanta? Or (recalling Jesse Jackson's presentation of Rosa Parks to the Convention) who, on that day in Montgomery, Alabama, in 1955, when Rosa Parks refused to move from the front of the bus, could have predicted that this would lead to a mass protest of black working people, and then would follow a chain of events that would shake the nation, startle the world, and transform the South?

But let's go back to the turn of the century. That a revolution should overthrow the Czar of Russia, in that most sluggish of semi-feudal empires, not only startled the most advanced imperial powers, but took Lenin himself by surprise and sent him rushing by train to Petrograd. Who could have predicted, not just the Russian Revolution, but Stalin's deformation of it, then Khrushchev's astounding exposure of Stalin, and recently Gorbachev's succession of surprises?

Or observe Germany after the first World War. There was a situation that fitted the Marxist model of social revolution most neatly—an advanced industrial society, with an educated, organized proletariat, a strong socialist-communist movement, a devastating economic crisis, and the still-fresh memory of a catastrophic war. Instead, the same conditions which might have brought revolution gave rise to that monstrous mutation, Nazism. Marxist scholars went into a dither of analysis to explain it.

I don't mean to pick on Marxists. But if they, probably the best equipped theoretically, the most committed and motivated to understand society, kept being bewildered, that suggests how impenetrable has been the mystery of social change in our time.

Who would have predicted the bizarre events of World War II—the Nazi-Soviet pact (those embarrassing photos of von Ribbentrop and Molotov shaking hands), and the German army rolling through Russia, causing colossal casualties, apparently invincible, and then being turned back at the gates of Leningrad, on the edge of Moscow, in the streets of Stalingrad, and then surrounded, decimated, and defeated, the strutting Hitler at the end huddled in his bunker, waiting to die?

And then the post-war world, taking a shape no one could have drawn in advance. The Chinese Communist Revolution, which Stalin himself had given little chance. And then the turns of that revolution: the break with the Soviet Union, the tumultuous and violent Cultural Revolution, and then another turnabout, with post-Mao China renouncing its most fervently-held ideas and institutions, making overtures to the West, cuddling up to capitalist enterprise, perplexing everyone.

No one foresaw the disintegration of the old Western empires happening so quickly after the war, or the odd array of societies that would be created in the newly independent nations, from the benign socialism of Nyerere's Tanzania to the madness of Idi Amin's Uganda.

Spain became an astonishment. A million died in the civil war which ended in victory for the Fascist Franco. I recall a veteran of the Abraham Lincoln Brigade telling me that he could not imagine Fascism being overthrown in Spain without another bloody war. After Franco was gone, and a parliamentary democracy, open to Socialists, Communists, anarchists, everyone, was established in Spain, that same man expressed his awe that it all happened without the fratricide so many thought was inevitable.

In other places too, deeply-entrenched regimes seemed to suddenly disintegrate—in Portugal, Argentina, the Philippines, Iran.

The end of World War II left two superpowers with their respective spheres of influence and control, vying for military and political power. The United States and the Soviet Union soon had 10,000 thermonuclear bombs each, enough to devastate the earth several times over. The international scene was dominated by their rivalry, and it was supposed that all affairs, in every nation, were affected by their looming presence.

Yet, the most striking fact about these superpowers in 1988 is that, despite their size, their wealth, their overwhelming accumulation of nuclear weapons, they have been unable to control events, even in those parts of the world considered to be their spheres of influence.

The Soviet Union, apparently successful in crushing revolts in Hungary and Czechoslovakia, has had to accommodate itself to the quick withdrawal of Yugoslavia from its orbit, the liberalization of Hungary in recent years, and the continued power of the Solidarity movement in Poland. Gorbachev's recent declarations about a new era in Soviet relations with the Warsaw Pact nations is a recognition of the inability of Soviet power to permanently suppress the desire for independence in neighboring countries.

The failure of the Soviet Union to have its way in Afghanistan, its decision to withdraw after almost a decade of ugly intervention, is the most striking evidence that even the possession of thermonuclear weapons does not guarantee domination over a determined population.

The United States has more and more faced the same reality.

It could send an army into Korea but could not win, and was forced to sign a compromise peace. It waged a full-scale war in Indochina, the most brutal bombardment of a tiny peninsula in world history, and yet was forced to withdraw. And in Latin America, after a long history of U.S. military intervention, with Yankee imperialism having its way again and again, this superpower, with all its wealth, all its weapons, found itself frustrated. It was unable to prevent a revolution in Cuba, and after succeeding in organizing a counter-revolution in Chile, could not prevent or overthrow a revolution in Nicaragua. For the first time, the nations of Latin America are refusing to do the bidding of *los norteamericanos*.

In the headlines every day, we see other instances of the failure of the presumably powerful over the presumably powerless: the inability of white South Africa to suppress the insurgency of the black majority; the inability of Israel, a nuclear power with formidable conventional arms, to contain the rebellion of Palestinians armed with stones in the West Bank and Gaza Strip.

This recitation of facts about 20th century history, this evidence of unpredictability in human affairs, might be rather dull, except that it does lead us to some important conclusions.

The first is that the struggle for justice should never be abandoned because of the apparent overwhelming power of those who have the guns and the money and who seem invincible in their determination to hold on to it. That apparent power has, again and again, proved vulnerable to human qualities less measurable than bombs and dollars: moral fervor, determination, unity, organization, sacrifice, wit, ingenuity, courage, patience—whether by blacks in Alabama and South Africa, peasants in El Salvador, Nicaragua, and Vietnam, or workers and intellectuals in Poland, Hungary, and the Soviet Union itself. No cold calculation of the balance of power need deter people who are persuaded that their cause is just.

The second is that, in the face of the manifest unpredictability of social phenomena, all of history's excuses for war and preparation for war—self-defense, national security, freedom, justice, stopping aggression—can no longer be accepted. Nor can civil war be tolerated. Massive violence, whether in war or internal upheaval, cannot be justified by any end, however noble, *because no outcome is sure.* Indeed, the most certain characteristic of any upheaval, like war or revolution, is its uncertainty. Any humane and reasonable person must conclude that if the ends, however desirable, are uncertain, and the means are horrible and certain, those means must not be employed.

This is a persuasive argument, it seems to me, to direct at all those people, whether in the United States or elsewhere, who are still intoxicated by the analogy of World War II, who still distinguish between "just and unjust wars" (a universal belief shared by the Catholic Church, the capitalist West, and the Soviet Union), and who are willing to commit atrocities, whether on Hiroshima or on Budapest, for some good cause.

It is also an argument that needs to be examined seriously by those who, in this world of vicious nationalism, terrible poverty, and the waste of enormous resources on militarism and war, understand the need for radical change.

Such change is needed, yet it must be accomplished without massive violence. This is the great challenge to human ingenuity in our time. It is a challenge to blacks in South Africa, to Palestinians in the Occupied Territories (both of whom seem to understand it), as well as to Americans and Russians disgusted with their governments' robbery of national resources for profit and power.

The recognition of unpredictability is troubling. But all we have lost are our illusions about power and about violence. What we gain is an understanding that the means we use to struggle for justice, even for revolutionary change, must scrupulously observe human rights. The lives and liberties of ordinary people must not be sacrificed, either by governments or by revolutionaries, certain that they know the end results of what they do, indifferent to their own ignorance.

Objections to Objectivity

I always started off, in the first class of the semester, whether I was teaching at Spelman College in Atlanta, or at Boston University, by saying something like this to the students: This is not an "objective" course. I will not lie to you, or conceal information from you because it is embarrassing to my beliefs. But I am not a "neutral" teacher. I have a point of view about war, about racial and sexual equality, about economic justice—and this point of view will affect my choice of subject, and the way I discuss it. I ask you to listen to my point of view, but I don't expect you to adopt it. You have a right to argue with me about anything, because, on the truly important issues of human life, there are no "experts." I will express myself strongly, as honestly as I can, and I expect you to do the same. I am not your only source of information, of ideas. Points of view different from mine are all around, in the library, in the press. Read as much as you can. All I ask is that you examine my information, my ideas, and make up your own mind.

1989

Before I became a professional historian, I had grown up in the dankness and dirt of New York tenements, had been knocked unconscious by a policeman while holding a banner in a demonstration, worked for three years in a shipyard, and dropped bombs for the U.S. Air Force. Those experiences, and more, made me lose all desire for "objectivity," whether in living my life, or writing history.

This statement is troubling to some people. It needs explanation (after which it may still be troubling, but for clearer reasons).

I mean by it that by the time I began to study history formally (I became a freshman at New York University at the age of 27, with a wife, our two-year-old daughter, and another child on the way) I knew I was not doing it because it was "interesting" or because it meant a solid, respectable career.

29

I had been touched in some way by the struggle of working people to survive (my mother and father, among others), by the glamor and ugliness of war, by the reading I had done trying to understand fascism, communism, capitalism, socialism. I could not possibly study history as a neutral. For me, history could only be a way of understanding and helping to change what was wrong in the world.

That did not mean looking only for historical facts to reinforce the beliefs I already held. It did not mean ignoring data that would change or complicate my understanding of society. It meant asking questions that were important for social change, questions relating to equality, liberty, peace, justice—but being open to whatever answers were suggested by looking at history.

I decided early that I would be biased in the sense of holding fast to certain fundamental values—the equal right of all human beings, whatever race, nationality, sex, religion, to life, liberty, the pursuit of happiness. The study of history was only worth devoting a life to if it aimed at those ideals. I would always be biased (leaning toward) those ends, stubborn in holding to them.

But I would be flexible, I hoped, in arriving at the "means" to achieve those ends. Scrupulous honesty in reporting on the past would be needed, because any decision on means had to be tentative, had to be open to change based on what one could learn from history. The values, ends, ideals I held, need not be discarded, whatever history disclosed. So there would be no incentive to distort the past, fearing that an honest recounting would hurt the desired ends.

The chief problem in historical honesty is not outright lying. It is omission or de-emphasis of important data. The definition of "important," of course, depends on one's values.

An example: I was still in college, studying history, when I heard a song by the folk-singer Woody Guthrie, called "The Ludlow Massacre," a dark, intense ballad, accompanied by slow, haunting chords on his guitar. It told of women and children burned to death in a strike of miners against Rockefeller-owned coal mines in southern Colorado in 1914.

My curiosity was aroused. In none of my classes in American history, in none of the textbooks I had read, was there any mention of the Ludlow Massacre or of the Colorado coal strike.

The labor movement interested me, perhaps because I had spent three years working in a shipyard, and helped to organize the younger shipyard workers, excluded from the tightly-controlled craft unions of the American Federation of Labor, into an independent union of our own. There was little in the college curriculum on labor history, so I undertook an independent course of study for myself.

That led me to a book, *American Labor Struggles*, written not by an historian but by an English teacher named Samuel Yellen. It had fascinating accounts of some ten labor conflicts in American history, most of which were unmentioned in my courses and my textbooks. One of the chapters was on the Colorado coal strike of 1913-1914.

I became fascinated by the sheer drama of that event. It began with the shooting of a young labor organizer on the streets of Trinidad, Colorado, on a crowded Saturday night, by two detectives in the pay of Rockefeller's Colorado Fuel & Iron Corporation. The miners, mostly immigrants speaking a dozen different languages, were living in a kind of serfdom in the mining towns where Rockefeller collected their rent, sold them their necessities, hired the police, and watched them carefully for any sign of unionization.

The killing of organizer Gerry Lippiatt sent a wave of anger through the mine towns. At a mass meeting in Trinidad, miners listened to a rousing speech by an 80-year-old woman named Mary Jones—"Mother Jones"—an organizer for the United Mine Workers: "The question that arises today in the nation is an industrial oligarchy...What would the coal in these mines and in these hills be worth unless you put your strength and muscle in to bring them...You have collected more wealth, created more wealth than they in a thousand years of the Roman Republic, and yet you have not any..."

The miners voted to strike. Evicted from their huts by the coal companies, they packed their belongings onto carts, onto their backs, and walked through a mountain blizzard to tent colonies set up by the United Mine Workers. There they lived for the next seven months, enduring hunger and sickness, picketing the mines to prevent strikebreakers from entering, and defending themselves against armed assaults. The Baldwin-Felts Detective Agency, hired by the Rockefellers to break the morale of the strikers, used rifles, shotguns, and a machine gun mounted on an armored car which roved the countryside and fired into the tents where the miners lived.

They would not give up the strike, however, and the Governor called in the National Guard. A letter from the vice-president of Colorado Fuel & Iron to John D. Rockefeller, Jr., in New York explained:

> You will be interested to know that we have been able to secure the cooperation of all the bankers of the city, who have had three or four interviews with our little cowboy governor, agreeing to back the State and lend it all funds necessary to maintain the militia and afford ample protection so our miners could return to work...Another mighty power has been rounded up on behalf of the operators by the getting together of fourteen of the editors of the most important newspapers in the state.

The National Guard was innocently welcomed to town by miners and their families, waving American flags, thinking that men in the uniform of the United States would protect them. But the Guard went to work for the operators. They beat miners, jailed them, escorted strikebreakers into the mines.

There was violence by the strikers. One strikebreaker

was murdered, another brutally beaten, four mine guards killed while escorting a scab. And Baldwin-Felts detective George Belcher, the killer of Lippiatt, who had been freed by a coroner's jury composed of Trinidad businessmen, was killed with a single rifle shot by an unseen gunman as he left a Trinidad drug store and stopped to light a cigar.

Still, the miners held out through the hard winter. But when spring came, someone had decided on more drastic action. Two National Guard companies stationed themselves in the hills above the largest tent colony, housing a thousand men, women, and children, near a tiny depot called Ludlow. On the morning of April 20, 1914, they began firing machine guns into the tents. While the men crawled away to draw fire, and shot back, the women and children crouched in pits dug into the tent floors. At dusk, the soldiers came down from the hills with torches, and set fire to the tents. The occupants fled.

The next morning, a telephone linesman, going through the charred ruins of the Ludlow colony, lifted an iron cot which covered a pit dug in the floor, and found the mangled, burned bodies of two women and eleven children. This became known as the "Ludlow Massacre."

I wondered why this extraordinary event, so full of drama, so peopled by remarkable personalities, went unmentioned in the history books. Why was this strike, which cast a dark shadow on the Rockefeller interests, and on corporate America generally, considered less important than the building by John D. Rockefeller of the Standard Oil Company, which was looked upon generally as an important and positive event in the development of American industry?

I knew that there was no secret meeting of industrialists and historians to agree to emphasize the admirable achievements of the great corporations, and ignore the bloody costs of industrialization in America. But I concluded that a certain unspoken understanding lay beneath the writing of textbooks and the teaching of history: that it would be considered bold, radical, perhaps even "Communist" to emphasize class struggle in the United States, a country where the dominant ideology emphasized the oneness of the nation—"We the people, in order to...etc. etc."— and the glories of the American system.

Very recently, a news commentator on a small radio station in Madison, Wisconsin, brought to my attention a textbook used in high schools all over the nation, published in 1986, entitled *Legacy of Freedom*, written by two high school teachers and one university professor of history, and published by a division of Doubleday and Company, one of the giant U.S. publishers. In a foreword, "To the Student," we find:

> *Legacy of Freedom* will aid you in understanding the economic growth and development of our country. The book presents the developments and benefits of our country's free enterprise economic system. You will read about the various ways that American business, industry, and agriculture have used scientific and technological advances to further the American free market system. This system allows businesses to generate profits while providing consumers with a variety of quality products from which to choose in the marketplace, thus enabling our people to enjoy a high standard of living.

In this overview, one gets the impression of a peaceful development, due to "our country's free enterprise economic system." Where is the long, complex history of labor conflict? Where is the human cost of this industrial development, in the thousands of deaths each year in industrial accidents, the hundreds of thousands of injuries, the short lives of workers (textile mill girls in New England dying in their 20s, after starting work at 12 and 13)?

The Colorado coal strike does not fit neatly into the pleasant picture created by most high school textbooks of the development of the American economy. Wouldn't a detailed account of that event raise questions in the minds of young people as it raised them in mine—questions that would be threatening to the dominant powers in this country, that would clash with the dominant ideology, that might get the questioners—whether teachers or principals, or school boards—into trouble, make them conspicuous, as pointed questions almost always point out the questioner to the rest of society?

Wouldn't the event undermine faith in the neutrality of government, the cherished belief (which I possessed through my childhood) that whatever conflicts there were in American society, it was the role of government to mediate them as a neutral referee, trying its best to dispense, in the words of the Pledge of Allegiance, "liberty and justice for all"?

Wouldn't the Colorado strike suggest that governors, that perhaps all political leaders, were subject to the power of wealth, and would do the bidding of corporations rather than protect the lives of poor, powerless workers?

A close look at the Colorado coal strike would discover that not only the state government of Colorado, but the national government in Washington—under the presidency of a presumed liberal, Woodrow Wilson—was also on the side of the corporations. While miners were being beaten, jailed, killed, by Rockefeller's detectives, or by his National Guard, the federal government did not act to protect the constitutional rights of its people. But when, after the Massacre, the miners armed themselves and went on a rampage of violence against the mine properties and mine guards, Wilson called out the federal troops to end the turmoil in southern Colorado.

And then, there was an odd coincidence. On the same day that bodies were discovered in the pit at Ludlow, Woodrow Wilson, responding to the jailing of a few American sailors in Mexico, ordered the bombardment of the Mexican port of Vera Cruz, landing ten boatloads of marines, occupying the city, killing over a hundred Mexicans. That same textbook, *Legacy of Freedom*, in that foreword "To the Student," says: "...*Legacy of Freedom* will aid you in understanding our country's involvement in foreign affairs, including our role in international conflicts and in peaceful and cooperative efforts of many kinds in many places."

Is that not a benign, misleading, papering-over of the history of American foreign policy?

A close study of the Ludlow Massacre would tell students something about our great press, the comfort we feel when picking up, not a scandal sheet or a sensational tabloid, but the sober, dependable *New York Times*. When the U.S. navy bombarded Vera Cruz, the *Times* wrote in an editorial: "...we may trust the just mind, the sound judgment, and the peaceful temper of President Wilson. There is not the slightest occasion for popular excitement over the Mexican affair; there is no reason why anybody should get nervous either about the stock market or about his business."

There is no *objective* way to deal with the Ludlow Massacre. There is the subjective (biased, opinionated) decision to omit it from history, based on a value system which doesn't consider it important enough. That value system may include a fundamental belief in the beneficence of the American industrial system (as represented by the passage quoted above from the textbook *Legacy of Freedom*). Or it may just involve a complacency about class struggle and the intrusion of government on the side of corporations. In any case, it is a certain set of values which dictates the ignoring of that event.

It is also a subjective (biased, opinionated) decision to tell the story of the Ludlow Massacre in some detail (as I do, in a chapter in my book *The Politics of History*, or in several pages in *A People's History of the United States*). My decision was based on my belief that it is important for people to know the extent of class conflict in our history, to know something about how hard working people had to struggle to change their conditions, and to understand the role of the government and the mainstream press in the class struggles of our past.

The claim of historians to "objectivity" has been examined very closely by Peter Novick, in his remarkable book, *That Noble Dream: The "Objectivity Question" and the American Historical Profession.*

Historians, for instance, have not been "objective" with regard to war.

In April 1917, just after the U.S. entered the European war, a group of eminent historians met in Washington to discuss "what History men can do for their country now." They set up the National Board for Historical Service in order to "aid in supplying the public with trustworthy information of historical or similar character."

One result was a huge outpouring of pamphlets written by historians with the purpose of instilling patriotism in the public. Thirty-three million copies of pamphlets written by historians were distributed. Most of them, according to a recent study of the role of historians in World War I propaganda by George T. Blakey, "reduced war issues to black and white, infused idealism and righteousness into America's role, and established German guilt with finality."

During World War II, the historian Samuel Eliot Morison criticized those historians who had expressed disillusionment with the First World War, saying they "rendered the generation of youth which came to maturity around 1940 spiritually unprepared for the war they had to fight...Historians...are the ones who should have pointed out that war does accomplish something, that war is better than servitude." Yet, in the same essay ("Faith of a Historian"), Morison declared his commitment to not instructing the present but to "simply explain the event exactly as it happened."

A number of historians, in the cold-war atmosphere of the 1950s, selected their facts to conform to the government's position. Two of them wrote a two-volume history of U.S. entry into World War II, in order, as they put it, to show "the tortured emergence of the United States of

America as leader of the forces of light in a world struggle which even today has scarcely abated..."

An honest declaration of their bias would have been refreshing. But, although they had access to official documents unavailable to others, they said in their preface: "No one, in the State Department or elsewhere, has made the slightest effort to influence our views." Perhaps not. But one of them, William Langer, was director of research for the CIA at one time, and the other, S.E. Gleason, was deputy executive secretary of the National Security Council.

Langer was also at one time a president of the American Historical Association. Another president of the AHA, Samuel Flagg Bemis, in his presidential address to that group in 1961, was very clear about what he wanted historians to do: "Too much...self-criticism is weakening to a people...A great people's culture begins to decay when it commences to examine itself...we have been losing sight of our national purpose...our military preparedness held back by insidious strikes for less work and more pay...Massive self-indulgence and massive responsibility do not go together...How can our lazy dalliance and crooning softness compare with the stern discipline and tyrannical compulsion of subject peoples that strengthen the aggressive sinews of our malignant antagonist?"

Daniel Boorstin, trying to please the House Committee on Un-American Activities, testified before it in 1953. He agreed with it that Communists should not be permitted to teach in American universities—presumably because they would be biased. As for Boorstin, he told the committee that he expressed his own opposition to communism in religious activities at the University of Chicago. And: "The second form of my opposition has been an attempt to discover and explain to students, in my teaching and in my writing, the unique virtues of American democracy."

After studying the "objectivity" of American historians, and noting how many slanted their work towards support for the United States, Peter Novick wondered if that kind of "hubris," the arrogance of national power, played a part in the ugly American intervention in Vietnam, and the cold war itself. He put it this way:

> If ill-considered American global interventionism had landed us in this bloodiest manifestation of the cold war, was it not at least worth considering whether the same hubris had been responsible for the larger conflict of which it was a part? Manifestly by the 1960s, the United States was overseeing an empire. Could scholars comfortably argue that it had been acquired, as had been said of the British Empire, "in a fit of absence of mind"?

In the 1960s, there was a series of tumultuous social movements, against racial segregation, against the Vietnam war, for equality among the sexes. This caused a reappraisal of the kind of history that supported war and the status quo, either directly, or by avoiding criticism in the name of "objectivity."

More and more books began to appear (or old books were brought to light) on the struggles of black people, on the attempts of women throughout history to declare their equality with men, on movements against war, on the strikes and protests of working people against their conditions—books which, while sticking closely to confirmed information, openly took sides, for equality, against war, for the working classes.

A group of radical historians, sometimes called "revisionists," became prominent in the profession. One of them, Jesse Lemisch, delivered a kind of manifesto for himself and others, challenging the orthodox historians:

> We exist, and people like us have existed throughout history, and we will simply not allow you the luxury of continuing to call yourselves politically neutral while you exclude all of this from your history. You cannot lecture us on civility while you legitimize barbarity. You cannot call apologetics "excellence" without expecting the most rigorous and aggressive of scholarly replies. We were at the Democratic

Convention, and at the steps of the Pentagon...And we are
in the libraries, writing history, trying to cure it of your
partisan and self-congratulatory fictions, trying to come a
little closer to finding out how things actually were.

This unapologetic activism of the 1960s (making history in the street, as well as writing it in the study) was
startling to many professional historians. And in the 1970s
and 1980s, it was accused by some scholars, and some organs of public opinion, of hurting the proper historical education of young people by its insistence on "relevance." As
part of the attack, a demand grew for more emphasis on
facts, on dates, on the sheer accumulation of historical information.

In May 1976, the *New York Times* published a series of
articles lamenting the ignorance of American students
about their own history. The *Times* was pained. Four leading historians whom it consulted were also pained. It
seemed students did not know that James Polk was president during the Mexican War, that James Madison was
president during the War of 1812, that the Homestead Act
was passed earlier than Civil Service reform, or that the
Constitution authorizes Congress to regulate interstate
commerce but says nothing about the cabinet.

We might wonder if the *Times*, or its historian-consul-
tants, learned anything from the history of this century. It
has been a century of atrocities: the death camps of Hitler,
the slave camps of Stalin, the devastation of Southeast Asia
by the United States. All of these were done by powerful
leaders and obedient populations in countries that had
achieved high levels of literacy and education. It seems that
high scoring on tests was not the most crucial fact about
these leaders, these citizens.

In the case of the United States, the killing of a million
Vietnamese and the sacrifice of 55,000 Americans were carried out by highly-educated men around the White House
who undoubtedly would have made impressive grades in

the New York Times exam. It was a Phi Beta Kappa, McGeorge Bundy, who was one of the chief planners of the bombing of civilians in Southeast Asia. It was a Harvard professor, Henry Kissinger, who was a strategist of the secret bombing of peasant villages in Cambodia.

Going back a bit in history, it was our most educated president, Woodrow Wilson, a historian himself, a Ph.D. and former president of Princeton, who bombarded the Mexican coast, killing more than one hundred innocent people, because the Mexican government refused to salute the American flag. It was Harvard-educated John Kennedy, author of two books on history, who presided over the American invasion of Cuba and the lies that accompanied it.

What did Kennedy or Wilson learn from all that history they absorbed in the best universities in America? What did the American people learn, in their high school history texts, to put up with these leaders?

Surely, how "smart" a person is on history tests like the one devised by the *Times*, how "educated" someone is, tells you nothing about whether that person is decent or indecent, violent or peaceful, whether that person will resist evil or become a consultant to warmakers, will become a Pastor Niemoller (a German who resisted the Nazis) or an Albert Speer (who worked for them), a Lieutenant Calley (who killed children at My Lai) or a Flight Officer Thompson (who tried to save them).

One of the two top scorers on the *Times* test was described as follows: "Just short of 20 years old, he lists outdoor activities and the Augustana War Games Club as constituting his favorite leisure-time pursuits, explaining the latter as a group that meets on Fridays to simulate historical battles on a playing board."

Everyone does need to learn history, the kind that does not put its main emphasis on knowing presidents and statutes and Supreme Court decisions, but inspires a new generation to resist the madness of governments trying to carve the world and our minds into their spheres of influence.

The Problem is Civil Obedience

There was a warrant out for my arrest in the fall of 1970, because I had been part of an anti-war demonstration at the Boston Army Base and was appealing my conviction and was supposed to show up in court. But I was also scheduled to engage in a debate on civil disobedience at Johns Hopkins University with the philosopher Charles Frankel. To skip the debate in order to dutifully obey the court order seemed absurd to me in the light of my argument for civil disobedience. So I flew to Baltimore, took part in the debate, flew home, and met my class in the morning, again feeling I could not obsequiously submit to authority when I was discussing with my class the necessity, at certain times, for defiance of the law. As I emerged from my class, two detectives introduced themselves (a university official was with them, having apparently been useful in looking up my class schedule) and escorted me to court just before I was dispatched briefly to the Charles Street jail. What follows is the gist of my remarks at Johns Hopkins. I apologize for the fact that, to get Charles Frankel's argument, you would have to find the book *Violence: The Crisis of American Confidence*, published by Johns Hopkins Press.

1972

I start from the supposition that the world is topsy-turvy, that things are all wrong, that the wrong people are in jail and the wrong people are out of jail, that the wrong people are in power and the wrong people are out of power, that the wealth is distributed in this country and the world in such a way as not simply to require small reform but to require a drastic reallocation of wealth. I start from the supposition that we don't have to say too much about this because all we have to do is think about the state of the world today and realize that things are all upside down.

Daniel Berrigan is in jail—a Catholic priest, a poet who opposes the war—and J. Edgar Hoover is free, you see. David Dellinger, who has opposed war ever since he was

this high and who has used all of his energy and passion
against it, is in danger of going to jail. The men who are
responsible for the My Lai massacre are not on trial; they are
in Washington serving various functions, primary and sub-
ordinate, that have to do with the unleashing of massacres,
which surprise them when they occur. At Kent State University four students were killed by the National Guard, but
it was students who were indicted. In every city in this
country, when demonstrations take place, the protestors,
whether they have demonstrated or not, whatever they
have done, are assaulted and clubbed by police, and then
they are arrested for assaulting a police officer.

Now I have been studying very closely what happens
every day in the courts in Boston, Massachusetts. You
would be astounded—maybe you wouldn't, maybe you
have been around, maybe you have lived, maybe you have
thought, maybe you have been hit—at how the daily
rounds of injustice make their way through this marvelous
thing that we call "due process." Well, that is my premise.

All you have to do is read the Soledad letters of
George Jackson, who was sentenced to one year to life of
which he spent ten years, for a 70-dollar robbery of a filling
station. And then there is the U.S. Senator who is alleged to
keep 185,000 dollars a year, or something like that, on the oil
depletion allowance. One is theft; the other is legislation.
Something is wrong, something is terribly wrong when we
ship 10,000 bombs full of nerve gas across the country, and
drop them in somebody else's swimming pool so as not to
trouble our own. So you lose your perspective after a while.
If you don't think, if you just listen to TV and read scholarly
things, you actually begin to think that things are not so
bad, or that just little things are wrong. But you have to get
a little detached, and then come back and look at the world,
and you are horrified. So we have to start from that supposition—that things are really topsy-turvy.

And our topic is topsy-turvy: civil disobedience. As
soon as you say the topic is civil disobedience, you are

saying our *problem* is civil disobedience. That is *not* our problem. Our problem is civil *obedience*. Our problem is the numbers of people all over the world who have obeyed the dictates of the leaders of their government and have gone to war, and millions have been killed because of this obedience. And our problem is that scene in *All Quiet on the Western Front* where the schoolboys march off dutifully in a line to war. Our problem is that people are obedient all over the world, in the face of poverty and starvation and stupidity, and war, and cruelty. Our problem is that people are obedient while the jails are full of petty thieves, and all the while the grand thieves are running the country. That's our problem.

We recognize this for Nazi Germany. We know that the problem there was obedience, that the people obeyed Hitler. People obeyed; that was wrong. They should have challenged and they should have resisted, and if we were only there, we would have showed them. Even in Stalin's Russia we can understand that; people are obedient, all these herd-like people.

But America is different. That is what we've all been brought up on. From the time we are this high, you tick off, one, two, three, four, five lovely things about America that we don't want disturbed very much.

But if we have learned anything in the past few years it is that these lovely things about America were never lovely. We have been expansionist and aggressive and mean to other people from the beginning. And we've been aggressive and mean to people in *this* country, and we've allocated the wealth of this country in a very unjust way. We've never had justice in the courts for the poor people, for black people, for radicals. Now how can we boast that America is a very special place? It is not that special. It really isn't.

Well, that is our topic, that is our problem: civil obedience. Law is very important. We are talking about obedience to law—law, this marvelous invention of modern times, which we attribute to Western civilization, and which we talk about proudly. the rule of law, oh, how wonderful, all these courses in Western civilization all over the land. Remember those bad old days when people were exploited by feudalism? Everything was terrible in the Middle Ages—but now we have Western civilization, the rule of law. *The rule of law has regularized and maximized the injustice that existed before the rule of law, that is what the rule of law has done.* Let us start looking at the rule of law realistically, not with that metaphysical complacency with which we always examined it before.

When in all the nations of the world the rule of law is the darling of the leaders and the plague of the people we ought to begin to recognize this. We have to transcend these national boundaries in our thinking. Nixon and Brezhnev have much more in common with one another than we have with Nixon. J. Edgar Hoover has far more in common with the head of the Soviet secret police than he has with us. It's the international dedication to law and order that binds the leaders of all countries in a comradely bond. That's why we are always surprised when they get together—they smile, they shake hands, they smoke cigars, they really like one another no matter what they say. It's like the Republican and Democratic parties, who claim that it's going to make a terrible difference if one or the other wins, yet they are all the same.

Basically it is us against them.

Yossarian was right. Remember, in *Catch-22?* He had been accused of giving aid and comfort to the enemy, which nobody should ever be accused of, and Yossarian said to his friend Clevinger: "The enemy is whoever is going to get you killed, whichever side they are on." But that didn't sink in, so he said to Clevinger: "Now you remember that, or one of these days you'll be dead." And remember? Clevinger, after a while, was dead. And we must remember that our enemies are not divided along national lines, that enemies are not just people who speak different languages and occupy different territories. Enemies are people who want to get us killed.

We are asked, "What if everyone disobeyed the law?" But a better question is, "What if everyone obeyed the law?" And the answer to that question is much easier to come by, because we have a lot of empirical evidence about what happens if everyone obeys the law, or if even most people obey the law. What happens is what has happened, what is happening. Why do people revere the law? And we all do; even I have to fight it, for it was put into my bones at an early age when I was a Cub Scout. One reason we revere the law is its ambiguity. In the modern world we deal with phrases and words that have multiple meanings, like "national security." Oh, yes, we must do this for national security! Well, what does that mean? Whose national security? Where? When? Why? We don't bother to answer those questions, or even to ask them.

The law conceals many things. The law is the Bill of Rights. In fact that is what we think of when we develop our reverence for the law. The law is something that protects us; the law is our rights—the law is the Constitution. Bill of Rights Day, essay contests sponsored by the American Legion on our Bill of Rights, that is the law. And that is good.

But there is another part of the law that doesn't get ballyhooed—the legislation that has gone through month after month, year after year, from the beginning of the Republic, which allocates the resources of the country in such a way as to leave some people very rich and other people very poor, and the other people scrambling like mad for what little is left. That is the law. If you go to a law school you will see this. You can quantify it by counting the big, heavy law books that people carry around with them and see how many law books you count that say "Constitutional Rights" on them and how many that say "Property," "Contracts," "Torts," "Corporation Law." That is what the law is mostly about. The law is the oil depletion allowance—although we don't have Oil Depletion Allowance

Day, we don't have essays written on behalf of the oil depletion allowance. So there are parts of the law that are publicized and played up to us—oh, this is the law, the Bill of
Rights. And there are other parts of the law that just do their
quiet work, and nobody says anything about them.

It started way back. When the Bill of Rights was first
passed, remember in the first administration of Washington? Great thing, the Bill of Rights passed! Big ballyhoo. At
the same time Hamilton's economic program was passed.
Nice, quiet, money to the rich—I'm simplifying it a little,
but not too much. Hamilton's economic program started it
off. You can draw a straight line from Hamilton's economic
program to the oil depletion allowance and to the tax write-
offs for corporations. All the way through—that is the history. The Bill of Rights publicized; economic legislation
unpublicized.

You know the enforcement of different parts of the
law is as important as the publicity attached to the different
parts of the law. The Bill of Rights, is it enforced? Not very
well. You'll find that freedom of speech in constitutional
law is a very difficult, ambiguous, troubled concept. Nobody really knows when you can get up and speak and
when you can't. Just check all of the Supreme Court decisions. Talk about predictability in a system—you can't predict what will happen to you when you get up on the street
corner and speak. See if you can tell the difference between
the Terminello case and the Feiner case, and see if you can
figure out what is going to happen. By the way, there is one
part of the law that is not very vague, and that involves the
right to distribute leaflets on the street. The Supreme Court
has been very clear on that. In decision after decision we are
affirmed an absolute right to distribute leaflets on the street.
Try it. Just go out on the street and start distributing leaflets.
And a policeman comes up to you and he says, "Get out of
here." And you say, "Aha!—Do you know *Marsh v. Alabama*, 1946?" That is the reality of the Bill of Rights. That's
the reality of the Constitution, that part of the law which is

portrayed to us as a beautiful and marvelous thing. And seven years after the Bill of Rights was passed, which said that "Congress shall make no law abridging the freedom of speech," Congress made a law abridging the freedom of speech. Remember? The Sedition Act of 1798.

So the Bill of Rights was not enforced. Hamilton's program was enforced, because when the whiskey farmers went out and rebelled, you remember, in 1794 in Pennsylvania, Hamilton himself got on his horse and went out there to suppress the rebellion to make sure that the revenue tax was enforced. And you can trace the story right down to the present day, what laws are enforced, what laws are not enforced. So you have to be careful when you say, "I'm for the law, I revere the law." What part of the law are you talking about? I'm not against the law. But I think we ought to begin to make very important distinctions about what laws do what things to what people.

And there are other problems with the law. It's a strange thing, we think that the law brings order. Law doesn't. How do we know that law does not bring order? Look around us. We live under the rule of law. Notice how much order we have? People say we have to worry about civil disobedience because it will lead to anarchy. Take a look at the present world in which the rule of law obtains. This is the closest to what is called anarchy in the popular mind—confusion, chaos, international banditry. The only order that is really worth anything does not come through the enforcement of law, it comes through the establishment of a society which is just and in which harmonious relationships are established and in which you need a minimum of regulation to create decent sets of arrangements among people. But the order based on law and on the *force* of law is the order of the totalitarian state, and it inevitably leads either to total injustice or to rebellion—eventually, in other words, to very great disorder.

We all grow up with the notion that the law is holy. They asked Daniel Berrigan's mother what she thought of her son's breaking the law. He burned draft records—one of the most violent acts of this century—to protest the war, for which he was sentenced to prison, as criminals should be. They asked his mother, who is in her eighties, what she thought of her son's breaking the law. And she looked straight into the interviewer's face, and she said, "It's not God's law." Now we forget that. There is nothing sacred about the law. Think of who makes laws. The law is not made by God, it is made by Strom Thurmond. If you have any notion about the sanctity and loveliness and reverence for the law, look at the legislators around the country who make the laws. Sit in on the sessions of the state legislatures. Sit in on Congress, for these are the people who make the laws which we are then supposed to revere.

All of this is done with such propriety as to fool us. This is the problem. In the old days things were confused, you didn't know. Now you know. It is all down there in the books. Now we go through due process. Now the same things happen as happened before, except that we've gone through the right procedures. In Boston a policeman walked into a hospital ward and fired five times at a black man who had snapped a towel at his arm—and killed him. A hearing was held. The judge decided that the policeman was justified because if he didn't do it he would lose the respect of his fellow officers. Well, that is what is known as due process—that is, the guy didn't get away with it. We went through the proper procedures and everything was set up. The decorum, the propriety of the law fools us.

This nation was founded on disrespect for the law, and then came the Constitution and the notion of stability which Madison and Hamilton liked. But then we found in certain crucial times in our history that the legal framework did not suffice, and in order to end slavery we had to go outside the legal framework, as we had to do at the time of the American Revolution. The unions had to go outside the legal framework in order to establish certain rights in the 1930s. And in this time, which may be more critical than the time of the Revolution or the Civil War, the problems are so horrendous as to require us to go outside the legal framework in order to make a statement, to resist, to begin to establish the kind of institutions and relationships which a decent society should have. No, not just tearing things up that you are not supposed to build up—you try to build up a people's park, that's not tearing down a system; you are building something up, but you are doing it illegally—the militia comes in and drives you out. That is the form that civil disobedience is going to take more and more, people trying to build a new society in the midst of the old.

But what about voting and elections? Civil disobedience—we don't need that much of it, we are told, because we can go through the electoral system. And by now we should have learned, but maybe we haven't, for we grew up with the notion that the voting booth is a sacred place, almost like a confessional. You walk into the voting booth and you come out and they snap your picture and they put it in the papers with a beatific smile on your face. You've just voted; that is democracy. But if you even read what the political scientists say—although who can?—about the voting process, you find that the voting process is a sham. Totalitarian states love voting. You get people to the polls and they register their approval. I know there is a difference,they have one party and we have two parties. We have one more party than they have, you see.

What we are trying to do, I assume, is really to get back to the principles and aims and spirit of the Declaration of Independence. This spirit is resistance to illegitimate authority and to forces that deprive people of their life and liberty and right to pursue happiness, and therefore under these conditions it urges the right to alter or abolish their current form of government—and the stress has been on abolish. But to establish the principles of the Declaration of Independence we are going to need to go outside the law, to stop obeying the laws that demand killing or that allocate wealth the way it has been done or that put people in jail for petty technical offenses and keep other people out of jail for enormous crimes. My hope is that this kind of spirit will take place not just in this country but in other countries because they all need it. People in all countries need the spirit of disobedience to the state, which is not a metaphysical thing but a thing of force and wealth. And we need a kind of declaration of interdependence among peoples in all countries of the world who are striving for the same thing.

The Supreme Court
is Not Supreme

The purpose of a course I gave for many years at Boston University, "Law and Justice in America," was to rid students of the idea that they could sit back passively and let the Constitution, the "rule of law," solve problems of injustice in our society. If I ever had such illusions myself, they disappeared during my years at Spelman College, in segregated Atlanta, and in the civil rights movement. To illustrate this, I had my Boston University students, as their major project for the semester, go out into the community and check the realities of justice against the word of the law. Some of their findings form the substance of this article, which I wrote for the *Civil Liberties Review*.

1973

The Supreme Court is not supreme. We are deceived by its regal appearance, its weighty volumes of reports, its exalted position in the scholarly mind and the public imagination. In the academy constitutional experts make meticulous studies of Supreme Court decisions, political scientists invent complex formulas to predict the votes of justices, and students are led to believe they can determine the state of civil liberties by reading the Constitution and the *U.S. Reports*.

But we are looking in the wrong place to assess the liberties of American citizens. And this error leads us to a false notion of what to do to make ourselves more free.

Both the source and the solution of our civil liberties problems are in the situations of every day: where we live, where we work, where we go to school, where we spend most of our hours. Our actual freedom is determined not by the Constitution or the Court, but by the power the policeman has over us on the street or that of the local judge

behind him; by the authority of our employers; by the
power of teachers, principals, university presidents, and
boards of trustees if we are students; by parents if we are
children; by children if we are old; by the welfare bureaucracy if we are poor; by prison guards if we are in jail; by
landlords if we are tenants; by the medical profession or
hospital administration if we are physically or mentally ill.

Freedom and justice are local things, at hand, immedi-
ate. They are determined by power and money, whose authority over our daily lives is much less ambiguous than
decisions of the Supreme Court. Whatever claim we Americans can make to liberty on the national level—by citing
elections, court decisions, the Bill of Rights—on the local
level we live at different times of the day in different feudal
fiefdoms where our subordination is clear.

Over the last four years my students, checking formal
constitutional rights against the realities of everyday life in
the Boston area, found these formal rights meaningless. If
they had confined themselves to the classroom, they might
have concluded that a whole string of Supreme Court decisions, from *Lovell v. Griffin* (1938) to *Flower v. U.S.* (1972),
have given us all the right to distribute literature to our
fellow citizens; they discovered instead that on the street it
is the police who decide if that right exists. The Supreme
Court is far away and cannot help at that moment when the
policeman says "Get going!" (or something more pungent).

In Lynn, Massachusetts, a few years ago, young radicals distributing leaflets in front of a high school were arrested for "promoting anarchy" (an old but still useful
Massachusetts statute). In Harvard Square a young man
with a cast on one arm was selling copies of a communist
newspaper. He was chased by police, beaten, and charged
with assault and battery (he spat on the policeman, the
latter testified; two eyewitnesses saw no spitting). It doesn't
matter that eventually the young people in the first case
were acquitted and the newspaper seller was found guilty;
all were deprived of freedom of expression at the time they

sought it.

Money is crucial for freedom of speech: with it one can buy prime television time; without it one communicates in the streets, subject to police power. Money is also essential for the constitutional guarantee against "unreasonable search and seizure." Police are more likely to ignore that guarantee when they are dealing with residents in poor neighborhoods than when suburban homeowners are involved.

When we are at work even the most progressive employer (with or without the collaboration of a union) has the final say over the most fundamental facts of our lives—the conditions of work, wages, whether indeed we will have a job. None of the much-hailed Supreme Court decisions on "equal protection of the laws" could reach down into the St. Johnsbury Trucking Company, where Charles Ramsey, a black man from Jamaica, had a clerical job. He was tormented and humiliated for his blackness by fellow employees, and was fired when he complained to the Massachusetts Commission Against Discrimination, which supported him but could not enforce its decision.

A large part of the time of young people is spent in school, where the hierarchy of power is clear: students are at the bottom, above them teachers, then deans, principals, presidents, and, above all, trustees and regents. "Tracking," whether overt or subtle, steers kids from poor families into vocational and secretarial schools and those from middle and upper class families toward college.

Censorship is common in schools. At Wellesley (Massachusetts) High School the showing of a Leroi Jones play with an interracial scene and four-letter vulgarities led to criminal prosecutions of teachers, the on-the-spot arrest of a student who repeated a forbidden word at a public meeting ("I know respectable families here in Wellesley that can't utter three sentences without the word 'fuck'"), and a general atmosphere of fear and punishment. Inside schools, as inside other institutions, the Constitution has no force.

The critical deprivations of liberty never get to the courts. They are settled "out of court" in the way that most such settlements are determined—by who is bigger and richer and can afford to wait. And so, for those people who can't buy a house, day-to-day living conditions depend on the landlord: how much rent they pay, whether repairs are made and whether the house is safe, and whether they need to worry about eviction. The home is vital to liberty: a property owner has privacy; a tenement pushes its occupants into the streets, into the jurisdiction of the police.

Only those who rebel at the out-of-court settlements by landlord, by employer, by husband or parents, or by police, will ever get to court—and not to the Supreme Court, but to the municipal court. My students, sitting week after week in Boston Municipal Court, Roxbury District Court, Dorchester District Court, were horrified. A young woman wrote: "You do a paper on constitutional due process—great, you're happy. Then you go into court, and all that falls apart."

The judge is monarch of the courtroom, deciding who can testify and who cannot, who is credible and who is not, who should be punished and who should go free, and how many years of a person's life should be spent behind bars. He appoints attorneys for the poor (my students found the average lawyer's consulting time with defendants was seven minutes—that's how feebly blows the trumpet of *Gideon* in the city court), and then decides the fate of each in a few minutes.

If the accused goes to prison (in 90 percent of the cases, this will occur without jury trial, a plea of guilty having been arranged by threat), he becomes a member of a totalitarian society, with daily humiliation, intermittent torture, and absolute control. "If we are what we are being treated as, then we should be shot," wrote one Massachusetts inmate.

These realities of wealth and power that determine our everyday liberties will remain unshaken by new statutes, new Justices, new leaders, new court decisions—unless counter-forces appear on the very ground where liberty is taken away: on the street, at home, in schools, hospitals, courts, prisons, places of work.

In Dorchester a particularly oppressive judge was shaken loose from his throne because a group called *tpf* ("the people first") organized the community over a two-year period to sign petitions, hold public hearings, and create an atmosphere in which the judicial administration had to act. In Somerville, residents of a low-income housing project exploded in angry demonstrations when a patrolman beat a young man to death in a paddy wagon, giving the police a bit of pause in future actions and implying that a forceful, permanent community presence around the police may be the only guarantee against police abuse.

Tenants organize against landlords, old people march on City Hall to demand reduced subway fares, and women organize against discriminatory employers; prisoners form unions, a Mental Patients Liberation Front emerges, and students barge into a trustees' meeting to get a faculty member's job back.

Perhaps we are beginning to learn that we cannot depend on paternal government, its bills of rights, its statutory reforms, its judicial rhetoric—but must support one another in an endless assertion of our own freedom. Lacking traditional forms of power and wealth, we can only create a force out of what we do have: our assembled selves, our ability to withhold our labor, to withdraw our compliance, to take hold cooperatively of the resources at hand. Thus we may be able to start right now to construct and continuously reconstruct the human relationships, the institutional arrangements, the ways of thinking that, close to home and even inside it, determine the real state of our liberties.

The Bill of Rights

I was one of the speakers at historic Faneuil Hall when the Civil Liberties Union of Massachusetts organized a celebration of the Bill of Rights. My speech probably had an air of sobriety, compared to two very funny people who also spoke that evening: the stand-up political satirist Barry Crimmins and the stand-out political writer Molly Ivins. Barry Crimmins looked out at the crowd and said something like: "We who speak at meetings like this are always accused of 'preaching to the converted.' Let me tell you: I love preaching to the converted." Truth is, converts need constant reinforcement, and also fresh inspiration so they can go out and add to our number.

1992

A few years back, a man high up in the CIA named Ray Cline was asked if the CIA, by its surveillance of protest organizations in the United States, was violating the free speech provision of the First Amendment. He smiled and said: "It's only an Amendment."

And when it was disclosed that the FBI was violating citizens' rights repeatedly, a high official of the FBI was asked if anybody in the FBI questioned the legality of what they were doing. He replied: "No, we never gave it a thought."

We clearly cannot expect the Bill of Rights to be defended by government officials. So it will have to be defended by the people.

If you do a bit of research into the origins of the Bill of Rights—and I had to do some because it is a job requirement of the historical profession—you will find that when the new government of the United States adopted the Bill of Rights in 1791, it did not do so with enthusiasm. The Bill of Rights was a political tool, to quiet down critics of the Constitution. A Bill of Rights on paper comforts people.

You don't have to take it seriously. Like that CIA man, you can smile, and say, they're only Amendments.

Well, in 1791, the first ten Amendments—the Bill of Rights—were added to the Constitution, and the First Amendment says, among other things: "Congress shall make no law...abridging the freedom of speech, or of the press..." Seven years later, in 1798, Congress passed a law abridging the freedom of speech and the press. It was the Sedition Act of 1798 and it provided jail sentences for people who criticized the government. A number of writers and speakers were imprisoned. They appealed to the court. Now we all learned in junior high school about checks and balances and how if Congress passes a law violating the Constitution we are very lucky to have the Supreme Court to check that and declare the law null and void. (I was always proud to know such a fancy phrase, "null and void.")

Well, the members of the Supreme Court, apparently having skipped junior high school, or perhaps understanding that the phrase "checks and balances" is just intended to satisfy schoolchildren—did not declare the Sedition Act null and void. Not at all. They said it was constitutional. You may ask: by what legal philosophy can Supreme Court justices explain how Congress can pass a law abridging the freedom of speech when the Constitution says Congress shall make no law abridging the freedom of speech? I could tell you how they did that, but it would take a while and cause indigestion. Let us just say that legal training is a wonderful thing, it enables you to explain the unexplainable, defend the indefensible, and rationalize the irrational.

It seems that especially in time of war or near-war (and in 1798 it was such a time) the First Amendment is ignored. You may have noticed that the year 1991 did not start with a celebration of the Bill of Rights, but with a war. And that the government established control over information and the mass media became tongue-tied with patriotic fervor and the First Amendment was bombed into oblivion.

It is a truism of our political culture: if you are at war for freedom and democracy, you can't have freedom and democracy. So, exactly when free speech is most needed, that is, when it is a matter of life and death for the young people about to be sent to the battlefield—exactly at such a moment the government declares it can be suspended.

In 1917, as armies of young men in Europe were slaughtering one another in the first World War, and the United States decided to send its own young men into the butchery, Congress passed the Espionage Act, and the Sedition Act, providing heavy sentences for those criticizing the war. The Supreme Court again put our junior high school lesson to shame: checks and balances? Not in wartime. Not when you need them. The great liberal Oliver Wendell Holmes himself wrote the opinions affirming the constitutionality of the Espionage Act, sending a man named Schenck to jail for distributing a leaflet criticizing the war and the draft. Two thousand people were prosecuted for speaking or writing against the war, including Eugene Debs, the great labor leader and Socialist.

There were ludicrous episodes in all that. A filmmaker who made a movie about the American Revolution was sent to prison for ten years because the movie portrayed the British as the enemy in the American Revolution, and now the British were our allies in the war. The name of the movie was "The Spirit of '76" and the title of the court case against the filmmaker was *U.S. v. Spirit of '76*.

And that case sums up the relationship of the government to the Bill of Rights: U.S. vs. Spirit of '76. It was the President of the United States, Harry Truman, who instituted loyalty oaths even before Joseph McCarthy waved his lists of Communists in the State Department. It was the Congress of the United States, Democrats as well as Republicans, that set up the House Un-American Activities Committee, and voted contempt citations against people who refused to bow down to that Committee. It was the Supreme Court that affirmed the convictions of the Holly-

wood Ten for invoking the First Amendment. It was Republicans and Democrats, it was all three branches of government, all of them swearing to uphold the Constitution of the
United States and all of them violating that oath.

A word about the Supreme Court. We now have nine
conservative justices, including one conservative woman
and one conservative black man. It's called American
pluralism. Many people have been depressed over this.
Frankly, I tried to get depressed, but didn't succeed. Sure,
it's better to have a liberal Supreme Court. But the Supreme Court at its most liberal has never been a dependable
protector of people's rights. One year it will say you have a
constitutional right to distribute leaflets in front of a super-
market. Another year it will say you can go to jail for that.
One year it will say: high school students have a right to
wear black armbands to protest a war. Another year it will
say: high school students don't have the right to put out
their own newspapers without censorship by the school
authorities. The Supreme Court, when it was liberal, affirmed that Japanese-Americans could be put in concentra-
tion camps because we were at war. The Supreme Court,
liberal or conservative, sworn to defend the Constitution,
has never been a bulwark against unconstitutional wars.

If it were left to the institutions of government, the Bill
of Rights would be left for dead. But someone breathed life
into the Bill of Rights. Ordinary people did it, by doing
extraordinary things. The editors and speakers who in spite
of the Sedition Act of 1798 continued to criticize the government. The black and white abolitionists who defied the
Fugitive Slave Law, defied the Supreme Court's Dred Scott
decision, who insisted that black people were human beings, not property, and who broke into courtrooms and
police stations to rescue them, to prevent their return to
slavery.

Women, who were arrested again and again as they
spoke out for their right to control their own bodies, or the
right to vote. Members of the Industrial Workers of the

World, anarchists, radicals, who filled the jails in California and Idaho and Montana until they were finally allowed to speak to working people. Socialists and pacifists and anarchists like Helen Keller and Rose Pastor Stokes, and Kate O'Hare and Emma Goldman, who defied the government and denounced war in 1917 and 1918. The artists and writers and labor organizers and Communists—Dalton Trumbo and Pete Seeger, and W.E.B. Du Bois and Paul Robeson, who challenged the congressional committees of the 1950s, challenged the FBI, at the risk of their freedom and their careers.

In the 1960s, the students of Kent State and Jackson State and hundreds of other campuses, the draft resisters and deserters, the priests and nuns and lay people, all the marchers and demonstrators and trespassers who demanded that the killing in Vietnam stop, the GIs in the Mekong Delta who refused to go out on patrol, the B-52 pilots who refused to fly in the Christmas bombing of 1972, the Vietnam veterans who gathered in Washington and threw their Purple Hearts and other medals over a fence in protest against the war.

And after the war, in the 70s and 80s, those courageous few who carried on, the Berrigans and all like them who continued to demonstrate against the war machine, the Seabrook fence climbers, the signers of the Pledge of Resistance against U.S. military action in Central America, the gays and lesbians who marched in the streets for the first time, challenging the country to recognize their humanity, the disabled people who spoke up, after a long silence, demanding their rights. The Indians, supposed to be annihilated and gone from the scene, emerging ghostlike, to occupy a tiny portion of the land that was taken from them, Wounded Knee, South Dakota. Saying: we're not gone, we're here, and we want you to listen to us.

These are the people, men, women, children, of all colors and national origins, who gave life to the Bill of Rights.

The Bill of Rights was expanded after the Civil War, with the passage of the 13th, 14th, and 15th Amendments, to apply to the states, to prevent them from keeping slavery, to require that they give all people, regardless of race or color, the equal protection of the laws. But these amendments were soon ignored, as blacks were kept in semi-slavery in the South, segregated, humiliated, beaten, lynched by mobs, unprotected by either the local police or the national government. For almost a hundred years after the 14th Amendment became law, every President, whether liberal or conservative, Republican or Democrat, violated his oath of office, his pledge to uphold the Constitution, by failing to enforce those Amendments. And the Supreme Court interpreted them so as to make them useless.

And so black people in the South, in the most dangerous towns and cities in the country, decided to give life to the 14th Amendment, at the risk of their own. They boycotted the buses in Montgomery, Alabama, they sat in at segregated lunch counters, they rode the buses as Freedom Riders, they marched through the streets of Albany, Georgia and Birmingham, demonstrated in Alabama, were arrested, set upon by dogs, knocked down by water hoses, beaten bloody by state troopers, and murdered. There were protests in 800 cities in the year 1963. And then the President acted, then Congress acted, then the Supreme Court acted. The 15th Amendment was now being enforced, only a hundred years late.

It is good to have a Bill of Rights, good to have a 14th and 15th Amendment. They are useful as standards. But it is disastrous to depend on them. Words have never been enough. Ask the authors of the Ten Commandments.

For many people there were not even words—not for working people, women, gays and lesbians, disabled people. The Bill of Rights says nothing about the right to work, to a decent wage, to housing, to health care, to the rights of women, to the right of privacy in sexual preference, to the rights of people with disabilities.

But we don't need permission from on high, words approved by the authorities, to tell us that certain truths are self-evident, as the Declaration of Independence put it. That we are all created equal, that we all have rights that cannot be taken from us, the rights to life, liberty, and the pursuit of happiness. And so working people went on strike thousands of times, were beaten and killed on the picket line, until they won an eight-hour day, and a bit of economic security. Women created a national movement that changed the consciousness of millions of people. Gays and lesbians, disabled people, organized, spoke up, declared: we exist, we must be paid attention to. And people began to pay attention.

We should look beyond the Bill of Rights to the UN's Universal Declaration of Human Rights, which says that all people, everywhere in the world, are entitled to work and decent wages, to holidays and vacations, to food and clothing and housing and medical care, to education, to child care and maternal care.

The guarantees of the Bill of Rights have little meaning so long as we have a class society with enormous differences of wealth and income. The rights of free speech and press depend on having the resources to use them. The right to legal counsel is different for rich and poor. The right to be free from unreasonable searches and seizures is different for a family living in a mansion and another living in a housing project, or out on the street.

In the real world, the fate of human beings is decided every day not by the courts, but out of court, in the streets, in the workplace, by whoever has the wealth and power. The redistribution of that wealth and power is necessary if the Bill of Rights, if any rights, are to have meaning.

The novelist Aldous Huxley once said: "Liberties are not given; they are taken." We are not given our liberties by the Bill of Rights, certainly not by the government which either violates or ignores those rights. We take our rights, as thinking, acting citizens.

And so we should celebrate today, not the words of the Bill of Rights, certainly not the political leaders who utter those words and violate them every day. We should celebrate, honor, all those people who risked their jobs, their freedom, sometimes their lives, to affirm the rights we all have, rights not limited to some document, but rights our common sense tells us we should all have as human beings. Who should, for example, we celebrate?

I think of Lillian Gobitis, from Lynn, Massachusetts, a seventh-grade student who, back in 1935, because of her religious convictions, refused to salute the American flag even when she was suspended from school.

And Mary Beth Tinker, a 13-year-old girl in Des Moines, Iowa, who in 1965 went to school wearing a black armband in protest against the killing of people in Vietnam, and defied the school authorities even when they suspended her.

An unnamed black boy, nine years old, arrested in Albany, Georgia, in 1961 for marching in a parade against racial segregation after the police said this was unlawful. He stood in line to be booked by the police chief, who was startled to see this little boy and asked him: "What's your name?" And he replied: "Freedom, freedom."

I think of Gordon Hirabayashi, born in Seattle of Japanese parents, who, at the start of the war between Japan and the United States, refused to obey the curfew directed against all of Japanese ancestry, and refused to be evacuated to a detention camp, and insisted on his freedom, despite an executive order by the President and a decision of the Supreme Court.

Demetrio Rodriguez of San Antonio, who in 1968 spoke up and said his child, living in a poor county, had a right to a good education equal to that of a child living in a rich county.

All those alternative newspapers and alternative radio stations and struggling organizations that have tried to give meaning to free speech by giving information that the mass media will not give, revealing information that the government wants kept secret.

All those whistleblowers, who risked their jobs, risked prison, defying their employers, whether the government or corporations, to tell the truth about nuclear weapons, or chemical poisoning.

Randy Kehler and Betsy Corner, who have refused to pay taxes to support the war machine, and all their neighbors who, when the government decided to seize and auction their house, refused to bid, and so they are still defending their right.

The 550 people who occupied the JFK Federal Building in Boston in protest when President Reagan declared a blockade of Nicaragua. I was in that group—I don't mind getting arrested when I have company—and the official charge against us used the language of the old trespass law: "failure to quit the premises." On the letter I got dropping the case (because there were too many of us to deal with) they shortened that charge to "failure to quit."

I think that sums up what it is that has kept the Bill of Rights alive. Not the President or Congress, or the Supreme Court, or the wealthy media. But all those people who have refused to quit, who have insisted on their rights and the rights of others, the rights of all human beings everywhere, whether Americans or Haitians or Chinese or Russians or Iraqis or Israelis or Palestinians, to equality, to life, liberty, and the pursuit of happiness. That is the spirit of the Bill of Rights, and beyond that, the spirit of the Declaration of Independence, yes, the spirit of '76: refusal to quit.

Second Thoughts
on the First Amendment

Here is a good example of how different are the media of the printed page and the speaker's platform. As I read this transcribed speech I gave, it doesn't read right. It lacks the dignity of the written essay (maybe I should say, of *others'* written essays!). It has the informal, carefree style of a talk given in summertime, in the library of the lovely Cape Cod town of Wellfleet, with both speaker and audience sun-tanned, relaxed, in a good mood, yet wanting to think seriously about the world.

1989

One of the things that I got out of reading history was to begin to be disabused of a notion of what democracy is all about. The more history I read, the more it seemed very clear to me that whatever progress has been made in this country on various issues, whatever things have been done for people, whatever human rights have been gained, have not been gained through the calm deliberations of Congress or the wisdom of presidents or the ingenious decisions of the Supreme Court. Whatever progress has been made in this country has come because of the actions of ordinary people, of citizens, of social movements. Not from the Constitution.

Think of whatever progress has been made in this country for economic justice. Obviously, not enough progress has been made for economic justice, looking around at this country. You have to look around. You have to walk through a whole city. If you walk through half a city you'll be mistaken. You have to walk through a *whole* city and you see the class structure in the United States, the hidden story of American prosperity.

So obviously we haven't made a lot of progress, but

we've made some progress. We got it down to an eight-hour day. We say an eight-hour day is a long day. People worked 12 and 14 and 16 hours and six days a week and seven days a week and then at a certain point we did get it down to an eight-hour day for at least a lot of people.

How was that done? It wasn't done through the Supreme Court. It wasn't done through Congress or through the President. There's nothing in the Constitution. An interesting thing about this much-touted Constitution is that it doesn't say anything about economic rights, at least not for people. It has something about freedom of contract, which is not an economic right for people but for corporations. But the Constitution has nothing about the right of people to breathe fresh air or to live in a decent house or to have medical care or to make enough money or to work not too many hours. There isn't anything about that in the Constitution. Whatever was gained in that way for working people was gained through an enormously rich, complex history of labor struggles in this country. This has been mostly ignored in the history books that have been written. When I was going through the history training process, being trained as a historian—you know, they snap a whip and hold up a book and you jump at it—I learned very little about labor history.

Then I began to read on my own about labor history. I was interested because I had spent three years working in a shipyard and I thought, hey, that's what interests me. I saw what hadn't been told about labor history, what magnificent events had taken place, what struggles people had gone through, what sacrifices, what risks, what courage had been shown, what had been demonstrated about the possibilities of what human beings can do once they get together, what people had gone through and what drama there was.

I wondered, where is Hollywood? Talk about drama! Hollywood is struggling to get a bit of drama into some stupid movies and here were some of the great dramatic events in American history. It wasn't there in our culture,

our books, our literature, on the screen. That's how whatever modicum of economic justice we have was gained.

What about the rights of women? Where is that in the
Constitution? People have been struggling to get something
into the Constitution about that, but there isn't. Whatever
has been gained for women, and something has been
gained for women in this country over the years, especially
in this century and especially maybe in the last ten or fifteen
years, but whatever has been gained has been gained
through the struggles of women themselves. Emma Goldman made this very clear when they were campaigning at
the beginning of the twentieth century for women's suf-
frage. She said, Look, I have nothing against women's suf-
frage. (She didn't want to alienate too many people. She had
already alienated almost everybody. She had seven friends
left. She didn't want to alienate them.) It's OK. It's good for
women to vote. Men vote, sure, why shouldn't women
vote? But look, don't kid yourself. The vote isn't going to
get you much. Look what it's gotten men! She said whatever women get they're going to have to get through direct
action against the circumstances of their oppression, against
the situations that oppress them in the home, in the workplace, in the community. They're going to have to act *directly*. Forget about constitutional amendments and law and
this and that. They may follow, but they will follow, not
lead.

The point I'm making about how things have happened, how things have changed, what progress has been
made, is perhaps no more vividly illustrated than in the
case of black people in this country. Yes, there is something
in the Constitution. There was something in the Constitution. What there was in the Constitution was bad. It affirmed slavery. That's why William Lloyd Garrison and the
New England Anti-Slavery Society went out to their annual
picnic and Garrison held up a copy of the Constitution and
held a match to it and burned the Constitution. They're
getting excited about the flag? How would they like *that*—

the Constitution? You remember guys used to burn their draft cards and politicians went apoplectic? What about burning the entire Constitution? He burned it because he said it's a covenant with hell.

Then finally, they did amend the Constitution. But they didn't amend it just because Congress thought one day, hey, it would be good to have equal rights. The 13th, 14th, and 15th Amendments came after an enormous struggle. I'm not just talking about the Civil War. I'm talking about the struggle that preceded and took place during the Civil War, the anti-slavery movement. It was that movement that created the atmosphere in which slavery could be done away with. It was that movement that created the pressure that pushed Abraham Lincoln to write that rather piddling document called the Emancipation Proclamation. It was piddling. It had great moral force, but if you read the language of the Emancipation Proclamation, it was so meager. He said, I now declare the slaves free in all the areas where we can't enforce it. In all the parts of the country where we can enforce it, the parts that are fighting with us, you don't have to worry about your slaves. They're still around.

But whatever happened then, the 13th Amendment, the 14th Amendment, resulted from the pressure of the anti-slavery movement, the atmosphere created by that enormous movement, which started out very small. And then when the 13th, 14th and 15th Amendments were passed, finally we had in the Constitution the obliteration of those terrible words that had made it a pro-slavery document, finally we had in the Constitution words about the equal protection of the laws and life, liberty, and so on. Property, yes, you can't leave that out. But when we had those noble words about equal protection of the laws, finally, and you can't deny people the right to vote on the basis of race, color, or previous condition of servitude, there it was, powerful, finally. The states can't do this to anybody. And everybody knows it was ignored.

So you have it in the Constitution. It didn't mean a thing. For 100 years it was ignored. The 14th Amendment didn't take on any meaning until black people rose up in the 1950s and 1960s in the South in mass movements in the hardest, toughest, most dangerous places for anybody to rise up anywhere. They created an excitement, an embarrassment to the national government that finally began to bring some changes. They made whatever words there were in the Constitution and the 14th Amendment have some meaning for the first time. That's what did it. Not the 14th Amendment. Not the Supreme Court. Some people date the civil rights movement from the 1954 decision of the Supreme Court, as if these nine guys suddenly looked at the 14th Amendment and said, hey, we haven't looked at this for a while. Maybe we ought to reconsider the 14th Amendment. Of course not. Aside from the fact that the cases would never have come before them if black people in the South hadn't taken enormous risks, including putting their lives on the line, to bring those cases before the Supreme Court.

But also, in 1954, the world was changing. We were in the Cold War and we were vying with the Soviet Union for the allegiance of the Third World and somebody discovered that the Third World is mostly non-white. It takes a while to discover that the world isn't mostly white. It's a shocking thing for white people to wake up one day and look at a map or statistics and find out, hey, we're a minority. The Supreme Court was very conscious that it would be a nice thing politically—I'm paraphrasing the Supreme Court. Attorney General Brownell argued as much before the Supreme Court: I think it would be helpful for us to have a nice, resounding statement about equality. But it was all that commotion that did it.

Then of course on the matter of foreign policy and the Constitution, the Constitution has a few things to say about foreign policy. That hardly means anything, as has become clearer and clearer. Who pays attention to the Constitution?

Does the President pay attention to the Constitution? The Constitution says it's *Congress* that declares war. Does the President pay any attention to that? He makes war when he wants to make war. Look at Korea, at Vietnam—who cares about what the Constitution says about who shall declare war? So if you're going to do anything in foreign policy, like if you're going to help stop a war, you're certainly not going to do it through the channels, through the Supreme Court or Congress.

They actually gave a Nobel Prize to Henry Kissinger for helping to stop the Vietnam War. It's enough to make you want to build 97 statues to Jean-Paul Sartre, who refused the Nobel Prize because he said it was a political prize. Imagine giving one of the architects of the war a prize for helping to stop the war because he signed that treaty at the end! But the war was not stopped by any of the formal institutions of government. In fact, the Supreme Court should have been—as we learned in elementary or junior high school—the guardian of the Constitution. When anybody does something that violates the Constitution, the Supreme Court is there to say, no, you can't do this. Some G.I.'s from the Vietnam War came up before the Supreme Court and said, we refuse to go to Vietnam because it's an unconstitutional war. You're the Supreme Court. O.K. The Supreme Court didn't rule against them. It just refused to hear the case. Wouldn't discuss it. The Supreme Court is great on little things. But you get to matters of life and death, it's nowhere.

So a movement had to be created in this country to stop the war. That's what happened. It bypassed the formal institutions of government, bypassed that sheepish, timorous, obsequious Congress that kept voting money for the war again and again, bypassed all the institutions and created an enormous commotion and tumult in the country and scared the President and Congress. You have to read the *Pentagon Papers* about what attention they were paying to public opinion and demonstrations and draft refusals to see how it affected their decisions about the war and their decision to start retrenching and not escalating the war any more.

That's what democracy is. It's what people do on behalf of human needs outside of, sometimes against, the law, even against the Constitution. When the Constitution was pro-slavery, the people had to go not just against the laws but against the Constitution itself in the 1850s when they were doing all that civil disobedience against the Fugitive Slave Act. People have to create disorder, which goes against what we learn about law and order and orderly society and "you must obey the law." Obey the law. Obey the law. It's a wonderful way of containing things.

I read an interview of Gertrude Scholtz-Klink. She was Chief of the Women's Bureau under Hitler. Did you know there was a Women's Bureau under Hitler? He was a great person for women's freedom. Scholtz-Klink made sure that women were doing what had to be done for the State. That was her job. She's still around, having fun. Somebody interviewed her about the Jewish policy of the Nazis and asked her how come people went along with that. She said, we always obey the law. Isn't that what you do in America? (That's a nasty thing to say.) We're just doing what you do. We obey the law. You obey the law. Even if you don't agree with the law personally, you still obey it. Otherwise, life would be chaos. We don't want chaos. We want order.

Before the Civil War some abolitionists said, criticizing William Lloyd Garrison: let's not create too much commotion. Let's do things more quietly. Yes, we're against slavery too, but you're really speaking too loud. Garrison replied, Slavery will not be overthrown without excitement, a tremendous excitement.

Now I'm finally going to get to the subject of my talk. This was all preliminary. Then I'll have a sort of post-thing, and about two minutes of my talk. I wanted to create a context. (We always claim that when we go on and on about something, we're creating a context.) I wanted to create a context for talking about the First Amendment because what I'm going to say about the First Amendment fits into this general theme about what democracy really is and whether democracy comes to you through the existence of these formal institutions or whether it requires all sorts of action and organization and risk and sacrifice and energy which goes on outside of the formal apparatus and which is engaged in by ordinary people. So, second thoughts on the First Amendment.

First thoughts on the First Amendment—I suppose we all have them. You read the First Amendment, hear about it, write essays for the *Reader's Digest* essay contest on Bill of Rights Day, how wonderful it is to have a First Amendment: "Congress shall make no law respecting the establishment of religion or abridging the free exercise thereof, abridging the freedom of speech or the press or the right of persons peaceably to assemble, to petition the government for redress of grievances..." It's a terrific amendment. It makes you feel good to have something like that in the Constitution as the basic law of the land, the highest law of the land. Its language is absolute. There are no exceptions in it, no buts or howevers. It's there. It's flat. It's absolute speech. It's fantastic.

But... (This is a good but. There are bad buts. I will only use good buts.) Freedom of expression does not depend on the First Amendment.

Let me give you an example. It took me a while to figure this out. It took me longer than it should have. I don't know exactly when I did, but I know one of the moments when I began to think about it very forcibly: when I was in the South teaching at Spelman College, which is a black college for women in Atlanta, Georgia. I was teaching there for seven years, from 1956 to 1963. It was an amazing time to be there. I could see my students move from a situation of absolute courtesy, politeness, quiet, order and suddenly burst out in the way things happen when people have despaired that anything will ever happen. At such a time you realize that you don't know anything about the way human beings are. You think you know what human beings are, by watching their external behavior. But you don't know what's going on inside people, what they're thinking and feeling, what they're holding back, how they're waiting for the right moment, how indignant they are, how wise they are. You look at people not doing anything and you put them down. People are not dopes. People have common sense. There's a reality there, and people feel it. They may not say anything about it. It may not be practical to say anything about it. But when the practical moment comes, things will happen.

So my students began to do these things. One day, a group of students who lived on campus came to my house and said, can we borrow your car. I was a great force in the civil rights movement: I had a car. I had a typewriter to type petitions on and really played a key role. I said, Where are you going? They said, we're going downtown. In fact, we have a question to ask of you. You teach constitutional law. I drew myself up to my full height, Oliver Wendell Holmes. We're going to distribute leaflets on Peachtree Street in downtown Atlanta against racial segregation.

You have to understand, Atlanta was as tightly segregated at that time as Johannesburg, South Africa. You didn't see a black mayor, black policemen, no such thing. It was like Johannesburg. We're going to go downtown, to the white downtown of Atlanta and we're going to distribute leaflets, we black students, against racial segregation. Do we have a constitutional right to do that?

The answer is easy for anybody who has studied constitutional law. There are a lot of ambiguities in Supreme Court decisions, a lot of things that are uncertain. But there's probably nothing in the Bill of Rights on which the members of the Supreme Court have been more firm than the right to distribute leaflets on the public street. That is clear. So the answer is an easy one: Yes. You have an absolute right to distribute leaflets on Peachtree Street.

Don't worry. That's what I might have said if I were a real idiot. I was half an idiot, but not a *real* idiot. So I had to say, yes, you do have a constitutional right, but what if a policeman comes up to you and says what policemen say in such situations (you can imagine what policemen say), something like, "Leave"?

Policemen have their principles. They don't like the sight of people distributing leaflets on certain subjects on public streets. Policemen will say, "Leave." So what do you do then? Obviously, the policeman is not quite aware of the Supreme Court decisions. So you say to the policeman, "Sir, I think I should inform you that I have an absolute constitutional right to do this, *Marsh vs. Alabama, 1946.*" At that point the situation is very clear. You have on your side the Constitution of the United States and the words of the Supreme Court. The policeman, all he has is his club and his gun. That stands for so much, tells so much about the difference between words on paper and the realities of power in the world.

What happened, of course, in the civil rights movement is that because black people in the South had so much experience with the realities of power, they didn't wait for the Supreme Court to come to a new decision on the right of black people to sit at lunch counters. In fact, the law was against that. If you studied constitutional law, you know that the law had been interpreted in 1883 for civil rights cases, and private entrepreneurs, restaurants and hotels, were not covered by the 14th Amendment. They could discriminate and you had no constitutional right to ask for service at a lunch counter or a hotel or any public place.

That was the situation when those kids sat-in in Greensboro, North Carolina, in February 1960. That was the situation for all the subsequent sit-inners in 1960 when sit-ins spread all over the South. They were going against the Constitution. But they won. They succeeded. One place after another, facing demonstrations and persistence and mass arrests and television pictures going around the world and embarrassment and boycotts and trouble, gave in. Constitution or no Constitution, whatever. Because what the movement did was to create a countervailing power to the policeman with a club and a gun. That's essentially what movements do: They create countervailing powers to counter the power which is much more important than what is written down in the Constitution or the laws.

Let me say a little about the First Amendment. It says, "Congress shall make no law abridging the freedom of speech." In 1791 the First Amendment was passed. Seven years later Congress passes a law abridging the freedom of speech: the Sedition Act of 1798 says that if you criticize the government you're going to be put in jail. No problem. The law's passed against the Constitution. The Supreme Court will take care of it, right? It goes into the courts. They try to put people in jail for violating the Sedition Act and criticizing the administration. The defendants cite the First Amendment and the Supreme Court justices say, "Sorry, the First Amendment doesn't apply." "Why not? It says Congress shall make no law abridging the freedom of speech. They're abridging our freedom of speech!"

You don't understand. People are really very thick. They think they can just read words and know what they mean. Why do people go to law school? To see what words *really* mean. How do you become a judge? You don't understand. You have to go behind those words, far behind those words, and you have to look: what does freedom of speech *mean?* It sounds talmudic, something you'd ask at Passover: What does freedom of speech *mean?* You have to go back to English Common Law. Let's see what freedom of speech means in English Common Law. Really, that was the argument of the judges.

English Common Law? We just had a revolution against England! It tells you a lot about revolutions. You had a revolution against England and your law's still English Common Law. English Common Law, you want to know what it is, you read Blackstone. Blackstone's put En-

glish Common Law into his Commentaries. He's codified it.
You read what he says about freedom of speech and Blackstone says: "Freedom of speech means no prior restraint."
That takes a little time. I can hear you thinking about it. I'm
thinking about it myself. "No prior restraint." In other
words, it means we can't stop you in advance from saying
what you want to say, but once you say it we can put you in
prison. That is the doctrine of no prior restraint.

I'm serious. Blackstone is serious. The Supreme Court
is serious. They're all serious. Down to the present day, that
is still what the First Amendment means. People are always
astonished to hear this. You might say, if you were just an
ordinary person: You're not going to stop me, but if I say it
I'll go to jail. If I know that, doesn't that stop me? Isn't that
prior restraint? You don't understand. There are big differences between common law and common sense.

So there we are with no prior restraint. That's why
Congress can pass laws abridging the freedom of speech.
And it does, as it did in the Sedition Act of 1798, and again
in World War I. They passed the Espionage Act in World
War I. The Espionage Act provides another lesson: don't
think you can tell a law from its title. Espionage Act, you
think, oh, good, we don't want espionage. Who wants espionage? It turns out the Espionage Act does have some
things on espionage. It also has other things, like "you can't
say this. You can't write this. You can't print this. You can't
publish this. You can't utter this." They love the word
"utter." I guess if you say it but don't utter it it's O.K. The
Act said you can't say or publish things that will discourage
recruitment in the armed forces of the United States.

They passed this in 1917. The United States had just
gone to war, joined that noble crusade, World War I, where
10 million men died in the battlefields and at the end of it
nobody knew why the war was fought. Not an atypical
situation for wars. At the end of it people look around at the
debris and say, "Hey, what happened here?" The Espionage Act is passed. You can't say things that would discour-

age recruitment or enlistment into the armed forces of the
United States. In other words, you can't speak against the
war. That's what it meant. Do not criticize the war.

Then it was tested. The Socialist Party was quite
strong in those early years of the twentieth century, really
strong. You had 57 Socialist locals in Oklahoma. I'm serious. It was a big movement. The Socialist Party was a big,
powerful movement. Schenk was a Socialist and distributed
leaflets against the draft and against the war. He was
brought in under the Espionage Act—which provided for
up to twenty years in prison, by the way—for saying things,
and he was convicted and he came up before the Supreme
Court. He said, "How about the First Amendment?"

The Supreme Court was unanimous: Oliver Wendell
Holmes wrote the decision. He has a great reputation, as an
intellectual, one of the really awesome figures in American
jurisprudence, intellectual history, etc. He actually corre-
sponded with Harold Laski. Anybody who corresponds
with Harold Laski must be O.K. Holmes writes the decision.
You've heard this decision before. You hear this all the time.
Your mother said it to you, your brother-in-law said it, who
knows? Somebody you heard said this: Freedom of speech
is fine, but you can't shout "Fire" in a crowded theater.
How many times have you heard that? That stops you. Who
wants to shout "Fire" in a crowded theater? That's the end
of it. That takes care of that.

Holmes, this brilliant man, gives this stupid metaphor,
this ridiculous analogy, that Schenk distributing a leaflet
criticizing our entrance into the war is like somebody getting up in a crowded theater and falsely shouting "Fire." A
clear and present danger to all these people. Who was creating a danger: Wilson by sending us into the war, or Schenk
by protesting against the war? Who started the fire that's
burning in Europe and that's killing all these people?
What's going on here? A unanimous Supreme Court ruled:
clear and present danger. So they send 900 people to prison.
They prosecute 2,000 and send 900 people to prison under

this Espionage Act, including Eugene Debs, the leader of
the Socialist Party. Oliver Wendell Holmes writes that decision, too. I'm more bitter against people who are revered as
liberals, people with three names. It was too much.

The First Amendment has always been shoved aside
in times of war or near war. 1798 was near war, 1917 was
war. In 1940 when the Smith Act was passed the country
was near war. The Smith Act was used against the Socialist
Workers Party and then against the Communist Party for
things that they said and wrote. In those trials against the
Communist and Socialist Workers Party the courtroom was
full with stuff the prosecution had brought in. What had
they brought in? Guns, bombs, dynamite fuses? No, they
brought in the works of Marx, Lenin, Engels, Stalin. That's
like a bomb. So people went to jail. For national security.

People fall prostrate before the words "national security." All you have to do is use the phrase "national security," and people say Oh, well, I'm sorry, do whatever you
want to if it's for national security. Take those famous
Watergate Nixon tapes. At one point Nixon says to Haldeman—he always had this plaintive tone—"What'll we do,
what'll we do, gee, what'll we say, what are they going to
ask us?" Haldeman said, "Say it's national security."

Just recently, a few years ago in Cambridge in my part
of the country, a debate was scheduled at Harvard between
Alan Dershowitz, who teaches at Harvard Law School, a
Zionist and strong supporter of Israel, and a guy named
Terzi, who's a representative of the PLO at the U.N. It was
going to be an interesting debate. PLO vs. Zionist at Harvard. The State Department went to court to prevent Terzi
from traveling from New York to Boston. Why? They were
worried about his safety on Amtrak? Why? Because the
appearance of this PLO guy in Boston and the things he
would say might undermine the foreign policy of the
United States. And the court upheld that. Terzi could not
come. National security is invoked to keep people out, to
keep out playwrights and Nobel Prizewinners and writers.

A lot of those writers overseas are socialists or communists or anarchists. Keep them out. National security.

The First Amendment, for a long, long time, only applied to the national government. It didn't apply to the states. The states could make any law they wanted abridging the freedom of speech. Georgia and Louisiana in the 1830s passed laws against the distribution of anti-slavery literature. Anybody who distributed anti-slavery literature in Georgia or Louisiana in the 1830s could be sentenced to death. It was not a violation of the First Amendment. It was perfectly constitutional because—here again you have to be careful reading things—the First Amendment says *Congress* shall make no law abridging the freedom of speech. It doesn't say Georgia shall make no law abridging the freedom of speech, or Louisiana. The states could do whatever they want.

We never reckoned with the cleverness of the Founding Fathers and all of those people who write these things. When the 14th Amendment was passed that might have put a little different thing on it, because the 14th Amendment was directed against states. The 14th Amendment says no *state* can deprive a person of life, liberty. Now we can act against the states. If we say no state can deprive a person of liberty without due process of law, maybe that should include freedom of the press, so now do we have protection for freedom of expression against the states? That came up in 1895 with some guy who wanted to speak on the Boston Common. They wouldn't let him speak on the Boston Common without getting a permit from the mayor. The mayor wouldn't give him a permit. He went to the court and they say, no, the 14th Amendment doesn't apply.

It wasn't until the 1920s, 1930s that this First Amendment was applied to the states. So we say, now the states cannot pass laws abridging the freedom of speech except that anybody who went out on the street to say something or distribute leaflets or make a speech was still at the mercy of the police and the state. Nothing new. There's such a thing as the police powers of the state, which the Supreme Court brings up again. The state has police powers and they're always balancing the First Amendment rights against the police powers of the state.

The First Amendment doesn't say that your right to free speech should be balanced against anything. But the Supreme Court has decided, and it's a very handy thing, that it should be balanced against the police powers of the state, just as on a national level it's balanced against national security interests. Whatever the state has to do to maintain order, etc. So some student who gets up in 1949 in Syracuse, New York, and makes a speech criticizing the government, gets arrested for it, goes up to the Supreme Court, and they say sorry, police powers of the state and so on.

What you're gathering from all this, I hope, is that the First Amendment is not as strong as it seems. I'm trying to hint at that. The First Amendment is not a bulwark for us. Interpretations by the courts are only the beginning of the problem, because the real problems come outside of court. Very few people get to court. Very few free speech cases are settled in court. Most free speech cases are settled out of court, that is, on the street or at work or in a family or at school, that is, they're settled in the world of reality. An enormous deal is made of what happens in the courts, what happens in the Constitution, Supreme Court decisions.

The Supreme Court has said that high school kids can be censored. They said that last year. High school authorities have a right to censor the things that high school kids write. What if the Supreme Court had said high school kids cannot be censored? How much of a difference would that make in the reality of a high school and the reality of the authoritarian atmosphere of a high school and the reality of the power of principals, of teachers, etc.? The fact that you have a constitutional right doesn't mean you're going to get that right. Who has the power there on the spot? The policeman on the street. The principal in the school. The employer on the job. The Constitution does not cover private employment. In other words, the Constitution does not cover most of reality. It doesn't cover most of the situations in which you need free speech.

Therefore, you have to get it yourself. You have to do what the IWW (Industrial Workers of the World) did. It did not have a constitutional right to go to the mining towns and lumber towns of the Northwest in the early twentieth century. The First Amendment had not been applied to the states. The states could do whatever they wanted to the IWW.

The IWW was not a legalistic outfit. Oh, no. Arrest our comrade, our brother? We'll send 100 people into that town. Arrest 100 people? We'll send 1000 people into that town. We're going to fill their jails, their streets, we're going to make life impossible for them until we can finally speak on that street corner. That's what the free speech fights were. Emma Goldman did the same thing. She had no constitutional right to speak in these places. She was arrested again and again, especially when she spoke about birth control or marriage. That's much more serious than war. She came back. She refused to be silenced. She came back and spoke, was arrested, and came back and spoke.

What did workers do, being fired for speaking their minds? They formed unions. That's a more important function of unions when unions were created than wages and hours, namely job security, that you can't be arbitrarily fired for something you said to your foreman. The union will come to your defense. The union will go out on strike if they fire you. People got together, collectivized, organized in order to defend themselves.

There are several problems about free speech that I haven't talked about which are very important. Suppose they didn't interfere with your right to speak. Suppose none of these restrictions, none of these Supreme Court interpretations, no policemen interfering with you, none of these interferences were there. There you are. Say what you want.

What resources do you have to speak out? How many people can you reach? You can get up on a soapbox and no one arrests you, and you reach 200 people. Procter and Gamble, which made the soapbox, has the money to go on the air and reach five million people.

Freedom of speech is not just a quality. It's a quantity. It's not a matter of do you have free speech, like: in America we have free speech. Just like, in America we have money. How *much* do you have? How much freedom of speech do you have? Do you have as much freedom of speech as Exxon?

There's a nice little radio station here (KGNU)—I'm sorry, it's a *great* radio station. I was there, which proves it's a good station. But they don't have a huge amount of free speech. They're not CBS, NBC, prime time. They're trying to reach some people in this area and doing a wonderful job, but they have to fight for a small audience. Resources. Who has the resources? The press is monopolized. Turn from CBS to NBC to ... it's all the same. Resources. The biggest problem with freedom of speech is the economic problem: who has the money to speak out, to reach large numbers of people?

There is an additional problem. Suppose you even overcame that and you had the resources. Now you could speak and reach a lot of people. What if you then were in that position and you had nothing to say? I'm serious. You had nothing to say because you didn't know anything, because all you knew was what the government told you, what CBS told you, and the other stations. What if you didn't have any alternate sources of information? If you don't have anything important to say, what's the point?

Freedom of speech is meaningless if the sources of information are controlled, if the government is putting pressure on the press to withhold information as it did in the Bay of Pigs, as in the CIA overthrow in Guatemala. The government used pressure to pull a *New York Times* reporter, Sidney Gruson, back from Guatemala because he was reporting the facts. They put pressure on to get another *Times* reporter, Ray Bonner, pulled back from El Salvador because they didn't like the stories he was printing. The government reaches in; the CIA hires people in the media to do their job for them.

It's not that the press is being taken advantage of by the government. Noam Chomsky said something about it in the book he coauthored with Edward Herman, *Manufacturing Consent*. It's a wonderful book, as is any book by Noam Chomsky. *Manufacturing Consent* is one of his latest. (You always hesitate to say what his latest book is because tomorrow another one will come out. I think it's one of his latest books.) He said you really can't totally blame the government for taking advantage of the press when the press seems to be so eager to be taken advantage of.

Information: where are you going to get it? The government is lying to you. I.F. Stone's first rule for newspaper people: governments lie. The government is lying to you and concealing information, deceiving you. You have to have something to say. You have to have independent sources of information.

This puts a tremendous responsibility on all of us. If we want freedom of expression, it's up to us. We have a tremendous job to do. We have to take risks. We have to speak out. The Constitution won't do it for us, nor the courts. We have to create social movements that create atmospheres of protection for people who will take risks and speak up. We have to create alternative sources of information. We have to do what was done during the Vietnam War when you had teach-ins outside the regular class curriculum, which had given people no information about Asia or Vietnam, just like the whole education system has given people no education about Latin America. This continent which is the closest to us, with which we have the most to do, we have the least education about. So we obviously need alternative sources of information. We need to do what was done during the Vietnam War: community newspapers, underground newspapers, alternate press services, such as Dispatch News Service, this little radical news service in Southeast Asia which broke the story of the My Lai massacre before anyone else did.

There's a lot of work to be done in speaking up. We need to create that excitement about the issues of the time, excitement about the war, excitement about the misallocation, the waste of the country's wealth on the military. We have to create excitement about homelessness and poverty and the class system in this country. We need information. People have to know things. People have to spread the information. That is a job that all of us have to be engaged in day by day. That's the job of democracy.

How Free is Higher Education?

I was invited to write this essay as part of a symposium on the university for the *Gannett Center Journal,* which was edited by Craig LaMay. There was going on at the time, and still is, I suppose, a hot national debate on multi-culturalism, on freedom of speech in the university, and conservatives were getting a little hysterical. I thought I would add my bit, based on my own experience in higher education.

1991

In early 1950, Congressman Harold Velde of Illinois, rising in the House of Representatives to oppose mobile library service to rural areas, told his colleagues: "The basis of communism and socialistic influence is education of the people."

That warning was uttered in the special climate of the Cold War, but education has always inspired fear among those who want to keep the existing distributions of power and wealth as they are.

In my 30 years of teaching—in a small southern college, in a large northeastern university—I have often observed that fear. And I think I understand what it is based on. The educational environment is unique in our society: it is the only situation where an adult, looked up to as a mentor, is alone with a group of young people for a protracted and officially sanctioned period of time and can assign whatever reading he or she chooses, and discuss with these young people any subject under the sun. The subject may be defined by the curriculum, by the catalog course description, but this is a minor impediment to a bold and imaginative teacher, especially in literature, philosophy, and the social sciences, where there are unlimited possibilities for free discussion of social and political issues.

That would seem to be an educational ideal—an arena

89

for free discussion, assuming a diversity of viewpoints from a variety of teachers, of the most important issues of our time. Yet it is precisely that situation, in the classrooms of higher education, which frightens the guardians of the status quo.

They declare their admiration for such freedom in principle, and suggest that radicals are insufficiently grateful for its existence. But when teachers actually *use* this freedom, introducing new subjects, new readings, outrageous ideas, challenging authority, criticizing "Western civilization," amending the "canon" of great books as listed by certain educational authorities of the past—then the self-appointed guardians of "high culture" become enraged.

Early in my teaching career I decided that I would make the most of the special freedom that is possible in a classroom. I would introduce what I felt to be the most important, and therefore the most controversial, questions in my classes.

When I was assigned, as a young professor at Spelman College, a college for black women in Atlanta, to teach a course in "Constitutional Law," I changed the course title to "Civil Liberties" and departed from the canonized recital of Supreme Court cases. I did not ignore the most important of these cases, but I also talked with the students about social movements for justice and asked what role these movements played in changing the environment within which Supreme Court decisions were made.

When I taught American history, I ignored the canon of the traditional textbook, in which the heroic figures were mostly presidents, generals, and industrialists. In those texts, wars were treated as problems in military strategy and not in morality; Christopher Columbus and Andrew Jackson and Theodore Roosevelt were treated as heroes in the march of democracy, with not a word from the objects of their violence.

I suggested that we approach Columbus and Jackson from the perspective of their victims, that we look at the magnificent feat of the transcontinental railroad from the viewpoint of the Irish and Chinese laborers who, in building it, died by the thousands.

Was I committing that terrible sin which is arousing the anger of today's fundamentalists—"politicizing the curriculum"? Is there any rendition of constitutional law, any recounting of American history that can escape being *political*—that is, expressing a political point of view? To treat Theodore Roosevelt as a hero (which is usually not done overtly, but in an expression of quiet admiration)—is that less "political" than pointing to his role as an early imperialist, a forerunner of a long string of crude U.S. interventions in the Caribbean?

I have no doubt that I was taking a political stand when, in the early 1960s, I expressed respect for my students who missed classes to demonstrate in downtown Atlanta against racial segregation. In doing that, was I being more political than the fundamentalist Allan Bloom, at Cornell, who pointed with pride to the fact that the students in his seminar on Plato and Aristotle stuck to their studies and refused to participate in the social conflict outside the seminar room?

In my teaching I never concealed my political views: my detestation of war and militarism, my anger at racial inequality, my belief in a democratic socialism, in a rational and just distribution of the world's wealth. To pretend to an "objectivity" that was neither possible nor desirable seemed to me dishonest.

I made it clear to my students at the start of each course that they would be getting *my* point of view on the subjects under discussion, that I would try to be fair to other points of view, that I would scrupulously uphold their right to disagree with me. (I understand that radicals too can become dogmatic and intolerant, or—and I'm not sure which is worse—recondite in their pretentious theorizing—but these are traits one finds at all points in the political spectrum.)

My students had a long experience of political indoc-
trination before they arrived in my class—in the family, in
high school, in movies and television. They would hear
viewpoints other than mine in other courses, and for the
rest of their lives. I insisted on my right to enter my opinions
in the marketplace of ideas, so long dominated by ortho-
doxy.

Surely the expression of "political views" (what is just,
or unjust? what can citizens do?) is inevitable in education.
It may be done overtly, honestly, or it may be there subtly.
But it is always there, however the textbook, by its very bulk
and dullness, pretends to neutrality, however noncommit-
tal is the teacher.

It is inevitably there because all education involves
selection—of events, of voices, of books—and any insistence
on one list of great books or great figures or great events is a
partial (in both senses of that term) rendering of our cultural
heritage.

Therefore it seems to me that the existence of free
expression in higher education must mean the opportunity
for many points of view, many political biases, to be presented to students. This requires a true pluralism of readings, ideas, viewpoints—a genuinely free marketplace of
thought and culture. Let both Shakespeare and Wole
Soyinka, Bach and Leonard Bernstein, Dickens and W.E.B.
Du Bois, John Stuart Mill and Zora Neale Hurston, Rem-
brandt and Picasso, Plato and Lao-tzu, Locke and Marx,
Aeschylus and August Wilson, Jane Austen and Gabriel
García Marquez, be available to students.

Such a free marketplace of ideas does not depend
essentially on "the curriculum." How many words have
been wasted moving those empty shells around the debat-
ing table! What is crucial is the content of those shells,
which depends on who the teachers are and who the students are. A thoughtful teacher can take a course labeled
"Western Civilization" and enlarge its content with an ex-
citing global perspective. Another teacher can be given a

course grandly called "World Civilization" and give the student an eclectic, limp recounting of dull events and meaningless dates.

That pluralism in thought that is required for truly free expression in higher education has never been realized. Its crucial elements—an ideologically diverse faculty, a heterogeneous student body (in class, race, sex—those words that bring moans from the keepers of the "higher culture")—have always been under attack from outside and from inside the colleges and universities.

McCarthyism—in which the corporate nature of academic institutions revealed itself in the surrender of university administrators to government inquisitors (see Ellen Schrecker's book, *No Ivory Tower: McCarthyism in the Universities*, for details)—was only the most flagrant of the attacks on freedom of expression. More subtle, more persistent, has been the control of faculty appointments, contract renewals, and tenure (inevitably with political considerations) by colleagues, but especially by administrators, who are the universities' links with the dominant forces of American society—the government, the corporations, the military.

Boston University, where I taught for many years, is not too far from typical, with its panoply of military and government connections—ROTC chapters for every military service, former government officials given special faculty posts, the board of trustees dominated by corporate executives, a president eager to curry favor with powerful politicos. Almost all colleges and universities are organized as administrative hierarchies in which a president and trustees, usually well connected to wealthy and important people in the outside world, make the critical decisions as to who may enjoy the freedom of the classroom to speak to the young people of the new generation.

Higher education, while enjoying some special privileges, is still part of the American system, which is an ingenious, sophisticated system of control. It is not totalitarian; what permits it to be called a democracy is that it allows apertures of liberty on the supposition that this will not endanger the basic contours of wealth and power in the society. It trusts that the very flexibility of a partially free system will assure its survival, even contribute to its strength.

Our government is so confident of its power that it can risk allowing some political choice to the people, who can vote for Democrats or Republicans but find huge obstacles of money and bureaucracy if they want an alternative. Our corporations are so wealthy that they can afford some distribution of wealth to a supportive middle class, but not to the 30 or 40 million people who live in the cellars of society.

The system can allow special space for free expression in its cultural institutions—the theater, the arts, the media. But the size of that space is controlled by money and power; the profit motive limits what is put on stage or screen; government officials dominate the informational role of the news media.

Yes, there is, indeed, a special freedom of expression in the academy. How can I at Boston University, or Noam Chomsky at MIT, or David Montgomery at Yale, deny that we have had more freedom in the university than we would have in business or other professions? But those who tolerate us know that our numbers are few, that our students, however excited by new ideas, go out into a world of economic pressures and exhortations to caution. And they know too that they can point to us as an example of the academy's openness to all ideas.

True, there is a tradition of academic freedom, but it is based on a peculiar unspoken contract. The student, in return for the economic security of a career and several years with some degree of free intellectual play, is expected upon graduation to become an obedient citizen, participating happily in the nation's limited pluralism (be a Republican or a Democrat, but please, nothing else).

The boundaries for free expression in the university, though broader than in the larger society, are still watched carefully. When that freedom is used, even by a small minority, to support social change considered dangerous by the guardians of the status quo, the alarm goes out: "The Communists are infiltrating our institutions"; "Marxists have taken over the curriculum"; "feminists and black militants are destroying classical education."

Their reaction approaches hysteria: "With a few notable exceptions, our most prestigious liberal arts colleges and universities have installed the entire radical menu at the center of their humanities curriculum," says Roger Kimball in his book *Tenured Radicals*. The shrillness of such alarms is never proportionate to the size of the radical threat. But the Establishment takes no chances. Thus J. Edgar Hoover and Joseph McCarthy saw imminent danger of communist control of the U.S. government; protectors of "the canon" see "tenured radicals" taking over higher education. The axes then get sharpened.

Yes, some of us radicals have somehow managed to get tenure. But far from dominating higher education, we remain a carefully watched minority. Some of us may continue to speak and write and teach as we like, but we have seen the axe fall countless times on colleagues less lucky. And who can deny the chilling effect this has had on other faculty, with or without tenure, who have censored themselves rather than risk a loss of promotion, a lower salary, a non-renewal of contract, a denial of tenure?

Perhaps, after all, Boston University cannot be considered typical, having had for 20 years probably the most authoritarian, the most politically watchful university president in the country. But although it is hard to match John Silber as an educational tyrant, he can be considered (I base this on spending some time at other universities) not a departure from the norm, but an exaggeration of it.

Have we had freedom of expression at Boston University?

A handful of radical teachers, in a faculty of over a thousand, was enough to have John Silber go into fits over our presence on campus, just as certain observers of higher education are now getting apoplectic over what they see as radical dominance nationwide. These are ludicrous fantasies, but they lead to attacks on the freedom of expression of those faculty who manage to overcome that prudent self-control so prominent among academics. At Boston it must have been such fantasies that led Silber to determinedly destroy the faculty union, which was a minor threat to his control over faculty. He handled appointments and tenure with the very political criteria that his conservative educational companions so loudly decry. In at least seven cases that I know of, where the candidates were politically undesirable by Silber's standards, he ignored overwhelming faculty recommendations and refused them tenure.

Did I have freedom of expression in my classroom? I did, because I followed Aldous Huxley's advice: "Liberties are not given; they are taken." But it was obviously infuriating to John Silber that every semester 400 students signed up to take my courses, whether it was "Law and Justice in America" or "An Introduction to Political Theory." And so he did what is often done in the academy; he engaged in petty harassments—withholding salary raises, denying teaching assistants. He also threatened to fire me (and four other members of the union) when we held our classes on the street rather than cross the picket lines of striking secretaries.

The fundamentalists of politics—the Reagans and Bushes and Helmses—want to pull the strings of control tighter on the distribution of wealth and power and civil liberties. The fundamentalists of law, the Borks and Rehnquists, want to interpret the Constitution so as to put strict limits on the legal possibilities for social reform. The fundamentalists of education fear the possibilities inherent in the unique freedom of discussion that we find in higher education.

And so, under the guise of defending "the common culture" or "disinterested scholarship" or "Western civilization," they attack that freedom. They fear exactly what some of us hope for, that if students are given wider political choices in the classroom than they get in the polling booth or the workplace, they may become social rebels. They may join movements for racial or sexual equality, or against war, or, even more dangerous, work for what James Madison feared as he argued for a conservative Constitution, "an equal division of property."

We have some freedom, but it needs to be guarded and expanded. As Bertolt Brecht wanted to say but was prevented from saying to his inquisitors of the House Committee on Un-American Activities: "We are living in a dangerous world. Our state of civilization is such that mankind already is capable of becoming enormously wealthy but as a whole is still poverty-ridden. Great wars have been suffered. Greater wars are imminent, we are told. Do you not think that in such a predicament every new idea should be examined carefully and freely?"

Just and Unjust Wars

Here, too, the generous reader will recognize and perhaps forgive the loose and easy style of an extemporaneous talk, in this case given at the University of Wisconsin in Madison, at the close of the U.S. military action in the Persian Gulf. It was a hard time for anti-war people, with most of the nation, whipped up by the government and the media in their customary collaboration, exultant at our "easy victory" (few American casualties; who cared about Iraqi casualties?). The anti-war minority was not silent; there were mass demonstrations in Washington, D.C., and other cities, thousands of small actions all around the country, some heroic refusals of participation by men and women in the military, who faced court-martial and prison. I tried to put the short war into a longer historical perspective.

1991

I think that the great danger of what has just happened in the Gulf is what the Administration wanted to happen, that is, to fight a war that would make war acceptable once more. The Vietnam War gave war a bad name. The people who lead this country have been trying ever since to find a war that would give war a *good* name. They think they've found it. I think it's important for us to sit back and think about not just the Gulf War, not just the Vietnam War, not just this or that war, but to think about the problem of war, of just and unjust war.

We've had all these conferences. All of you who were around at the beginning of the twentieth century remember the Hague Conferences and the Geneva Conferences of the 1930s limiting the techniques of war. The idea was: you can't do away with war, all you can do is make war more humane. Einstein went to one of these conferences. I don't know how many of you know that. (We like to bring up things that people don't know. What is scholarship, any-

99

way?) Einstein was horrified at World War I, as so many were, that great war for democracy, for freedom, to end all wars, etc. Ten million men die on the battlefield in World War I and nobody, at the end of it, understands why, what for. World War I gave war a bad name. Until World War II came along.

But Einstein was horrified by World War I. He devoted a lot of time to thinking and worrying about it. He went to this conference in Geneva. He thought they were discussing disarmament, to do away with the weapons of war and therefore to prevent war. Instead, he found these representatives of various countries discussing what kinds of weapons would be suitable and what kind of weapons needed to be prohibited. What were good weapons and bad weapons, just weapons and unjust weapons? Einstein did something which nobody ever expected. He was a very private man. He did something really uncharacteristic: he called a press conference. The whole international press came, because Einstein was, well, he was Einstein. They came, and he told this press conference how horrified he was by what he had heard at the international conference. He said, "One does not make wars less likely by formulating rules of warfare. War cannot be humanized. It can only be abolished."

We still have that problem of just and unjust wars, of unjust wars taking place and then another war takes place which looks better, has a better rationale, is easier to defend, and so now we're confronted with a "just" war and war is made palatable again. Right now the attempt is to put Vietnam behind us, that unjust war, and now we have a just war. Or at least a quick one, a real smashing victory.

I had a student a few years ago who was writing something about war. I don't know why a student of mine should write about war. But she said, "I guess wars are like wines. There are good years and bad years. But war is not like wine. War is like cyanide. One drop and you're dead." I thought that was good.

What often is behind this business of "we can't do anything about war" and "war, be realistic, accept it, just try to fool around with the edges of it" is a very prevalent notion that you sometimes hear a lot when people begin discussing war. Fourteen minutes into any discussion of war someone says, "It's human nature." Don't you hear that a lot? You just get a group of people together to discuss war and at some point somebody will say, "It's human nature." There's no evidence of that. No genetic evidence. No biological evidence. All we have is historical evidence. And that's not evidence about our nature—that's evidence about circumstance.

There's no biological evidence, no genetic evidence, no anthropological evidence. What is the anthropological evidence? You look at these "primitive" tribes, as anthropologists call them, look at what they do, and say, "Ah, these tribes are fierce." "Ah, these tribes are gentle." It's just not clear at all.

And what about history? There's a history of wars and also a history of kindness. But it's like the newspapers and the historians. They dwell on wars and cruelty and the bestial things that people do to one another. They don't dwell a lot on the magnificent things that people do for one another in everyday life again and again. It seems to me it only takes a little bit of thought to realize that if wars came out of human nature, out of some spontaneous urge to kill, then why is it that governments have to go to such tremendous lengths to mobilize populations to go to war? It seems so obvious, doesn't it? They really have to work at it. They have to dredge up enormous numbers of reasons. They have to inundate the airwaves with these reasons. They have to bombard people with slogans and statements and then, in case people aren't really persuaded, they have to threaten them. If they haven't persuaded enough people to go into the armed forces, then they have to draft them.

Of course the persuasion into the armed forces also includes a certain amount of economic persuasion. You make sure you have a very poor underclass in society so that you give people a choice between starving or going into the military. But if persuasion doesn't work and entice-ments don't work, then anybody who doesn't want to sign up for the draft or who goes into the army and decides to leave is going to be court-martialed and go to prison. They have to go to great lengths to get people to go to war. They work very hard at it.

What's interesting also is that they have to make moral appeals. That should say something about human nature, if there is something to be said about human nature. It suggests that there must be some moral element in human nature. Granted that human beings are capable of all sorts of terrible things and human beings are capable of all sorts of wonderful things. But there must be something in human beings which makes them respond to moral ap-peals. Most humans don't respond to appeals to go to war on the basis of "Let's go and kill." No, "Let's go and free somebody. Let's go and establish democracy. Let's go and topple this tyrant. Let's do this so that wars will finally come to an end." Most people are not like Theodore Roose-velt. Just before the Spanish-American War, Theodore Roo-sevelt said to a friend, "In strict confidence" (you might ask then, how did I get hold of it; you read all these public letters that now appear and they all start "in strict confi-dence")—"I should welcome almost any war, for I think this country needs one." Well. No moral appeal there. Just we *need* a war.

You may know that George Bush, when he entered the White House, took down the portrait that Reagan had put up there to inspire him. It was a portrait of Calvin Coolidge, because Reagan knew that Calvin Coolidge was one of the most inspiring people in the history of this country. Coo-lidge had said: "The business of America is business." Bush took down the portrait of Calvin Coolidge and put up the portrait of Theodore Roosevelt. I don't want to make too much of this. But I will. What Theodore Roosevelt said,

Bush might just as well have said. Bush wanted war.

Every step in the development of this Persian Gulf War indicated, from the moment that the invasion of Kuwait was announced, everything that Bush did fits in perfectly with, the fact that Bush wanted war. He was determined to have war. He was determined not to prevent this war from taking place. You can just tell this from the very beginning: no negotiations, no compromise, no—what was that ugly word?—linkage. Bush made linkage the kind of word that made you tremble. I always thought that things were linked naturally. Everybody was linked, issues were linked. I thought that even the countries in the Middle East were somehow linked, and that the issues in the Middle East were somehow linked. No negotiations, no linkage, no compromise. He sends Baker to Geneva, and people got excited. Baker's going to meet the Foreign Minister of Iraq, Tariq Aziz, in Geneva. What are they going to do? Bush says, no negotiations. Why are you going? Are you a frequent flyer? Amazing. No negotiations, right up to the end.

Who knows if Saddam Hussein in any of those little overtures that were made, I don't know how serious he was or what would have happened, but the fact is there were overtures that came, yes, even from Saddam Hussein, and they were absolutely and totally neglected. One came from a member of the Foreign Service of the United States who brought it personally from the Middle East and gave it to Scowcroft. No response, no response at all. Bush wanted this war.

But, as I said, there aren't a lot of people, fortunately, like Theodore Roosevelt and Bush. Most people do not want war. Most people, if they are going to support a war, have to be given reasons that have to do with morality, with right and wrong, with justice and lack of justice, with tyranny and opposing tyranny. I think it's important to take a look at the process by which populations are, as this one was in a very short time, brought to support a war. On the eve of war, you remember, before January 15, the surveys all showed that the American public was divided half and half, 46 percent to 47 percent on the issue of "should we use force to solve this problem in the Middle East." Half and half.

Of course, after the bombs started falling in Iraq, it suddenly became 75 percent and then 80 percent in favor of war. What is this process of persuasion? It seems to me we should take a look at the elements of that, because it's important to know that, to be able to deal with it and talk to people about it, especially since that 80 or 85 percent or now they report 89.3 percent, whatever, must be a very shallow percentage. It must be very thin, I think. It must be very temporary and can be made more temporary than it is. It must be shallow because half of those people before the bombs fell did not believe in the use of force. Public opinion, as we know, is very volatile. So to look at the elements by which people are persuaded is to begin to think about how to talk to at least that 50 percent and maybe more, who are willing to reconsider whether this war was really just and necessary and right, and whether any war in our time could be just and necessary and right.

I think one of the elements that goes into this process of persuasion is the starting point that the U.S. is a good society. Since we're a good society, our wars are good. If we're a good society, we're going to do good things. We do good things at home. We have a Bill of Rights and color television. There are lots of good things you can say if you leave out enough.

It's like ancient Athens. Athens goes to war against Sparta. Athens must be on the right side because Athens is a better society than Sparta. Athens is more cultured. Sure, you have to overlook a few things about ancient Athens, like slavery. But still, it really is a better society. So the notion is that Athens fighting Sparta is probably a good war. But you have to overlook things, do a very selective job of analyzing your own society, before you come to the conclusion that yours is so good a society that your unadorned goodness must spill over into everything you do, including everything you do to other people abroad.

What is required, it seems to me, is, in the case of the U.S. as the good society doing good things in the world, simply to look at a bit of history. It's only if you were born yesterday and also if today you don't look around very sharply that you can come to the conclusion that we are so good a society that you can take the word of the government that any war we get into will be a right and a just war. But it doesn't take too much looking into American history to see that we have a long history of aggression.

Talk about naked aggression. A long history of naked aggression. How did we get so big? We started out as a thin band of colonies along the East Coast and soon we were at the Pacific and expanding. It's not a biological thing, that you just expand. No. We expanded by force, conquest, aggression. Sure it says, "Florida Purchase" on those little maps that we used to have in elementary school, a map with colors on them. Blue for Florida Purchase, orange for Mexican Cession. A purchase. Just a business deal. Nothing about Andrew Jackson going into Florida and killing a number of people in order to persuade the Spaniards to sell Florida to us. No money actually passed hands, but we'll ignore that.

The Mexican Cession. Mexico "ceded" California and Colorado and New Mexico and Arizona. They ceded all of that to us. Why? Good neighbors. Latin American hospitality. Ceded to us. There was a war, a war which we provoked, which President Polk planned for in advance, as so many wars are planned for in advance. Then an incident takes place and they say, Oh, wow, an incident took place. We've got to go to war. That was also a fairly short war and a decisive victory and soon we had 40 percent of Mexico. And it's all ours. California and all of that.

Why? Expansion. I remember how proud I was way back when I first looked at that map and saw "Louisiana Purchase." It doubled the size of my country, and it was just by purchase. It was an empty space. We just bought it. I really didn't learn anything, they didn't tell me when they gave me that stuff in history class, that there were Indians living in that territory. Indians had to be fought in battle after battle, war after war. They had to be killed, exterminated. The buffalo herds, their means of subsistence, had to be destroyed, they had to be driven out of that territory so that the Louisiana Purchase could be ours.

Then we began to go overseas. There was that brief period in American history, that honest moment in a textbook where it has a chapter called "The Age of Imperialism." 1898 to 1903. There, too, we went into Cuba to save the Cubans. We are always helping people. Saving people from somebody. So we went in and saved the Cubans from Spain and immediately planted *our* military bases and *our* corporations in Cuba. Then there was Puerto Rico. A few shells fired and Puerto Rico is ours.

In the meantime Teddy Roosevelt is swimming out into the Pacific after the Philippines. Not contiguous to the U.S. People didn't know that. McKinley didn't know where the Philippines were. And Senator Beveridge of Indiana said, "The Philippines not contiguous to the U.S.? Our Navy will make it contiguous." Ours is a history of expansion, aggression, and it continues.

We become a world power. Around 1905-1907, the first books began to appear about American history which used that phrase, "America as a world power." That in fact was what we intended to do, to become a world power. It took World War I and then World War II. We kept moving up and the old imperial powers were being shoved out of the way, one by one.

Now the Middle East comes in. In World War II Saudi Arabia becomes one of our friendly places. The English are being pushed out more and more, out of this oil territory. The Americans are going to come in. Of the "Seven Sisters," the seven great oil corporations, five of them will be American, maybe one will be British. In the years after World War

II, of course, the Soviet Union is the other great power, but we are expanding and our influence is growing and our military bases are spreading all over the world and we are intervening wherever we can to make sure that things go our way.

In 1940-41, at the beginning of World War II, Henry Luce, a very powerful man in America, the publisher of *Life* and *Time* and *Fortune* and the maker of presidents, wrote an article called "The American Century," anticipating that this coming century is going to be ours. He said, "This is the time to accept wholeheartedly our duty and our opportunity as the most vital and powerful nation in the world and in consequence to exert upon the world the full impact of our influence. For such purposes as we see fit and by such means as we see fit." He was not a shy man. So we proceeded.

While it was thought that anti-communism, rivalry with the Soviet Union, the other great superpower, was the central motive for the American foreign policy in the post-war period, I think it's more accurate to say that the problem was not communism, the problem was independence from American power. It didn't matter whether a country was turning communist or not, it mattered that a country was showing independence and not falling in line with what the United States conceived of as its responsibility as a world power. So in 1953 the government in Iran was overthrown and Mossadeq came into power. He was not a communist but a nationalist. He was a nationalist also because he nationalized the oil. That is intolerable. Those things are intolerable, just like Arbenz in Guatemala the following year. He's not a communist. Well, he's a little left of center, maybe a few socialist ideas, maybe he talks to communists. But he's not a communist. He's nationalized United Fruit lands. That's intolerable.

Arbenz offers to pay United Fruit. That proves that he's certainly not a real revolutionary. A real revolutionary wouldn't give a cent to United Fruit... I wouldn't. I've always considered myself a real revolutionary because I wouldn't pay a cent to anybody like United Fruit. He offered to pay them the price of their land, the price that they had declared for tax purposes. Sorry. That won't do. So the CIA goes to work and overthrows the Arbenz government.

And the Allende government in Chile also. Not a communist government, a little marxist, a little socialist, quite a lot of civil liberties and freedom of the press, but more independent of the United States than the other governments of Chile. A government that's not going to be friendly to Anaconda Copper and ITT and other corporations of the U.S. that have always had their way in Latin America. That's the real problem.

That history of expansion, of intervention, is not even to talk about Vietnam, Laos, Cambodia. Not to talk about all the tyrants that we kept in power, of all the aggressions not just that we committed but that we watched other countries commit as we stood silently by because we approved of those aggressions.

Until Noam Chomsky brought up the name of East Timor into public discussion nobody had even heard of it. The CIA had heard of East Timor. Anyway, Indonesia went into East Timor and killed huge numbers of people. The invasion, occupation, and brutalization that Saddam Hussein committed in Kuwait was small in comparison to the enormous bloodshed in East Timor, done by Indonesia, our friend, and with military hardware supplied by the U.S.

The record of the U.S. in dealing with naked aggression in the world, looking at a little bit of history, is so shocking, so abysmal, that nobody with any sense of history could possibly accept the argument that we were now sending troops into the Middle East because the U.S. government is morally outraged at the invasion of another country. That Bush's heart goes out to the people of Kuwait, who are suffering under oppression. Bush's heart never went out to the people of El Salvador, suffering under the oppression of a government which we were supplying with arms again and again. Tens and tens and tens of thousands of people were being killed. His heart never went out to those people. Or the people in Guatemala, again, whose government we were supplying with arms. It's a long list.

The moral appeal of war is based on people's forgetting of history and on the ability of the mass media and the Administration to obliterate history, certainly not to bring it up. You talk about the responsibility of the press. Does the press have no responsibility to teach any history to the people who read its newspaper columns? To remind people of what has happened five, ten, twenty, forty years ago? Was the press also born yesterday and has forgotten everything that happened before last week? The press complained about military censorship. The big problem was not military censorship. The problem was self-censorship.

Another element in this process of persuasion is to create a Manichean situation, good versus evil. I've just talked about the good, us. But you also have to present the other as total evil. As the only evil. Granted, Saddam Hussein is an evil guy. I say that softly. But he is. No question about it. Most heads of government are. But if you want to bring a nation to war against an evil person, it's not enough to say that this person is evil. You have to cordon him off from all the other tyrants of the world, all the other evil leaders of government in order to establish that this is the one tyrant in the world whom we have to get. He is responsible for the trouble in the world. If we could only get him, we could solve our problems, just as a few years ago if we could only get Noriega, we could solve the drug trade problem. We got Noriega—and obviously we've solved the drug trade problem. But the demonization is necessary, the creation of this one evil shutting out everything, Syria, Turkey, Egypt, Saudi Arabia, not letting people be aware of them.

I didn't see the media paying any attention to this, to the latest reports of Amnesty International, in which, if you read the 1990 report of Amnesty International, they have a few pages on each country. There are a lot of countries. A

few pages on Iraq, Iran, Turkey, Syria, Saudi Arabia, Kuwait, Israel. You look through those pages and all those
countries that I have just named show differences in degree,
but the same pattern of treatment of people who are dis-
senters, dissidents, troublemakers in their own country. In
Israel, of course, it's the Palestinians. Israel has a more free
atmosphere in the non-occupied, but in the occupied territories, Israel behaves the way Saudi Arabia behaves towards its own people and the way Syria and Turkey do.
You see the same pattern in the Amnesty International reports, the same words appearing again and again. Imprisonment without trial. Detention without communication
with the outside. Torture. Killing. For all of these countries.
But if you want to make war on them, you single one out,
blot out the others, even use them as allies and forget about
their record. Then you go in. You persuade people that
we're against tyranny, aren't we? We're against brutality,
aren't we? *This* is the repository of all the evil that there is in
the world. There are times when people talked that way.
Why are we at war? We've got to get him. We've got to get
Saddam Hussein. What about the whole world? Saddam
Hussein. Got to get him.

I would like to get him. I would like to get all of them.
But I'm not willing to kill 100,000 or 500,000 or a million
people to get rid of them. I think we have to find ways to get
rid of tyrants that don't involve mass slaughter. That's our
problem. It's very easy to talk about the brutality. Governments are brutal, and some governments are more brutal
than others. Saddam Hussein is particularly brutal. But in
addition, Saddam Hussein uses chemical weapons and gas.
That kept coming up. I remember Congressman Stephen
Solarz, the great war hawk of this period: Saddam Hussein
used gas, used chemical warfare. True, ugly and brutal. But
what about us? We used napalm in Vietnam. We used
Agent Orange, which is chemical warfare. I don't know
how you characterize napalm. We used cluster bombs in
Iraq. Cluster bombs are not designed to knock down mili-

tary hardware. They are anti-personnel weapons which shoot out thousands of little pellets which embed themselves in people's bodies. When I was in North Vietnam during the Vietnam War I saw x-rays of kids lying in hospital beds showing the pellets in the various organs of their bodies. That's what cluster bombs are. But gas? No. Chemical weapons? No. Napalm, yes. Cluster bombs, yes. White phosphorus, yes. Agent Orange, yes. They're going to kill people by gas. We're going to kill people by blowing them up. You can tell who is the cruel wager of war and who is the gentlemanly wager of war.

You can persuade people of that if you simply don't mention things or don't remind people. Once you remind people of these things they remember. If you remind people about napalm they remember. If you say, the newspapers haven't told you about the cluster bombs, they say, oh yes, that's true. People aren't beastly and vicious. But then information is withheld from them and the American population was bombarded the way the Iraqi population was bombarded. It was a war against us, a war of lies and disinformation and omission of history. That kind of war, overwhelming and devastating, waged here in the U.S. while that war was waged over there.

Another element in this process of persuasion is simply to take what seems like a just cause and turn it into a just war. Erwin Knoll used that terminology. I have used that terminology, and both of us, because we're so wise, seem to come to the same conclusions. That is, that there's this interesting jump that takes places between just cause and just war. A cause may be just: yes, it's wrong for Saddam Hussein to go into Kuwait, it's wrong for this and that to happen. The question is, does it then immediately follow that if the cause is just, if an injustice has been committed, that the proper response to that is war? It's that leap of logic that needs to be absolutely avoided.

North Korea invades South Korea in 1950. It's unjust, it's wrong. It's a just cause. What do you do? You go to war.

You wage war for three years. You kill a million Koreans. And at the end of the three years, where are you? Where you were before. North Korea is still a dictatorship. South Korea is still a dictatorship. Only a million people are dead. You can see this again and again, jumping from a just cause to an overwhelming use of violence to presumably rectify this just cause, which it never does.

What war does, even if it starts with an injustice, is multiply the injustice. If it starts on the basis of violence, it multiplies the violence. If it starts on the basis of defending yourself against brutality, then you end up becoming a brute.

You see this in World War II, the best of wars. The war that gave wars such a good name that they've used it ever since as a metaphor to justify every war that's taken place since then. All you have to do in order to justify war is to mention World War II, mention Churchill, mention Munich. Use the word "appeasement." That's all you need to take the glow of that good war and spread it over any ugly act that you are now committing in order to justify it.

Yes, World War II had a good cause. A just cause against fascism. I volunteered. I don't like to admit that I was in World War II, for various reasons. I like to say, "I was in a war." I suppose I admit that I was in World War II so that people won't think I mean the Spanish-American War. I volunteered for World War II. I went into the Air Force and became a bombardier and dropped bombs on Germany, France, Czechoslovakia, Hungary. I thought it was a just cause. Therefore you drop bombs.

It wasn't until after the war that I thought about this and studied and went back to visit a little town in France that I and a lot of the Air Force had bombed, had in fact dropped napalm on. The first use of napalm that I know of was this mission that we flew a few weeks before the end of World War II. We had no idea what it was. They said it was a new type of thing we were carrying, the bomb. We went over and just bombed the hell out of a few thousand German soldiers who were hanging around a town in France waiting for the war to end. They weren't doing anything. So we obliterated them and the French town near Bordeaux on the Atlantic coast of France.

I thought about that, about Dresden, the deliberate bombing of civilian populations in Germany, in Tokyo. Eighty, ninety, a hundred thousand people died in that night of bombing. This was after our outrage, our absolute outrage at the beginning of World War II when Hitler bombed Coventry and Rotterdam and a thousand people were killed. How inhuman to bomb civilian populations. By the end of World War II we had become brutalized. Hiroshima, Nagasaki, and even after that.

I have a friend in Japan who was a teenager when the war ended. He lived in Osaka. He remembers very distinctly that on August 14, five days after the bomb dropped on Nagasaki, the Japanese agreed to surrender on August 15. After Nagasaki it was very clear that they were about to surrender in a matter of days, but on August 14 a thousand planes flew over Japan and dropped bombs on Japanese cities. He remembers on August 14, when everybody thought the war was over, the bombers coming over his city of Osaka and dropping bombs. He remembers going through the streets and the corpses and finding leaflets also dropped along with the bombs saying: the war is over.

Just causes can lead you to think that everything you then do is just. I suppose I've come to the conclusion that war, by its nature, being the indiscriminate and mass killing of large numbers of people, cannot be justified for any political cause, any ideological cause, any territorial boundary, any tyranny, any aggression. Tyrannies, aggressions, injustices, of course they have to be dealt with. No appeasement. They give us this multiple choice: appeasement or war. Come on! You mean to say between appeasement and war there aren't a thousand other possibilities? Is human ingenuity so defunct, is our intelligence so lacking that we cannot devise ways of dealing with tyranny and injustice without killing huge numbers of people? It's like the police. The only way you can deal with a speeding motorist is to take him out of his car and beat the hell out of him, fracture his skull in ten different places? It's a sickness of our time. Somehow at the beginning of it is some notion of justice and rightness. But that process has to be examined, reconsidered. If people do think about it they have second thoughts about it.

One of the elements of this process of persuasion is simply to play on people's need for community, for national unity. What better way to get national unity than around a war? It's much easier, simpler, quicker. And of course it's better for the people who run the country to get national unity around a war than to get national unity around giving free medical care to everybody in the country. Surely we could build national unity. We could create a sense of national purpose. We could have people hanging out yellow ribbons for doing away with unemployment and homelessness. We could do what is done when any group of people decides and the word goes out and the air waves are used to unite people to help one another instead of to kill one another. It can be done. People do want to be part of a larger community. Warmakers take advantage of that very moral and decent need for community and unity and being part of a whole and use it for the most terrible of purposes. But it can be used the other way, too.

The reason I've gone into what I see as this process of persuasion and the elements of persuasion is that I think that all of them are reversible. History can be learned. Facts can be brought in. People can be reminded of things that they already know. People do have common sense when they are taken away briefly from this hysteria which is created in the time of war. I can only describe what's happened in these last few months as a kind of national hysteria created by the government and collaborated with by the media. When you have an opportunity to lift the veil of that hysteria and take people away from under it and talk to people, then you see the possibilities. When you appeal to people's sense of proportion: What is more important? What is it that we have to do? People know that there are things that have to be done to make life better. People know that the planet is in danger, and that is far more serious than getting Saddam Hussein out of Kuwait ever was. Far more serious.

I think people also may be aware in some dim way—every once in a while I think of it, and I imagine other people must think of it, too—that here it is, 1991, and we're coming to the end of the century. We should be able, by the end of this century, to eliminate war as a way of solving international disputes. We should have decided, people all over the world, that we're going to use our energy and our resources to create a new world order, but not *his* new world order, not the new world order of war, but a new world order in which people help one another, in which we divide the enormous wealth of the world in humane and rational ways. It's possible to do that. So I'm just suggesting that we think about that. I feel that there's something that needs to be done and something that *can* be done and that we can all participate in it.

Terrorism Over Tripoli

This angry little piece, intended as an Op-Ed column somewhere, found no takers, as I recall. To me, the Reagan
administration's senseless bombing of Tripoli (I hope I'm not suggesting that there is such a thing as a *sensible* bombing) represented
so many other events, smaller and larger, in which innocent people were sacrificed for a "principle"—leaving the rest of us bewildered about what this principle was. I also wanted to expand the
use of the word "terrorism" to include the actions of governments,
which are guilty of it far more often, and on an infinitely larger
scale, than tiny bands of revolutionaries or nationalists.

1986

"Indeed, I tremble for my country when I reflect that
God is just." Thomas Jefferson wrote that in *Notes from
Virginia*.

Those words came to mind as I listened to the an-
nouncement from our government that it had bombed the
city of Tripoli.

We live in a world in which we are asked to make a
moral choice between one kind of terrorism and another.
The government, the press, the politicians, are trying to
convince us that Ronald Reagan's terrorism is morally superior to Muammar Khadafi's terrorism.

Of course, we don't call our actions "terrorism," but if
terrorism is the deliberate killing of innocent people to
make a political point, then our bombing a crowded city in
Libya fits the definition as well as the bombing—by whoever did it—of a crowded discotheque in Berlin.

Perhaps the word "deliberate" shows the difference:
when you plant a bomb in a discotheque, the death of
bystanders is deliberate; when you drop bombs on a city, it
is accidental. We can ease our conscience that way, but only
by lying to ourselves. Because, when you bomb a city from

117

the air, you know, absolutely *know*, that innocent people will die.

That's why Defense Secretary Weinberger, reaching for morality (his reach will never be long enough, given where he stands) talked of the air raid being organized in such a way as to "minimize" civilian casualties. That meant there would inevitably be civilian casualties, and Weinberger, Shultz, and Reagan were willing to have that happen, to make their point, as the discotheque terrorists were willing to have that happen, to make theirs.

In this case, the word "minimize" meant only about a hundred dead (the estimate of foreign diplomats in Tripoli), including infants and children, an eighteen-year-old college girl home for a visit, an unknown number of elderly people. None of these were terrorists, just as none of the people in the discotheque were responsible for whatever grievances are felt by Libyans or Palestinians.

Even if we assume that Khadafi was behind the discotheque bombing (and there is no evidence for this), and Reagan behind the Tripoli bombing (the evidence for this is absolute), then both are terrorists, but Reagan is capable of killing far more people than Khadafi. And he has.

Reagan, Weinberger, Secretary of State Shultz, and their admirers in the press and in Congress are congratulating themselves that the world's most heavily-armed nation can bomb with impunity (only two US fliers dead, a small price to pay for psychic satisfaction) a fourth-rate nation like Libya.

Modern technology has outdistanced the Bible. "An eye for an eye" has become a hundred eyes for an eye, a hundred babies for a baby. The tough-guy columnists and anonymous editorial writers (there were a few courageous exceptions) who defended this, tried to wrap their moral nakedness in the American flag. But it dishonors the flag to wave it proudly over the killing of a college student, or a child sleeping in a crib.

There is no flag large enough to cover the shame of

killing innocent people for a purpose which is unattainable. If the purpose is to stop terrorism, even the supporters of the bombing say it won't work; if the purpose is to gain respect for the United States, the result is the opposite: all over the world there is anger and indignation at Reagan's mindless, pointless, soulless violence. We have had presidents just as violent. We have rarely had one so full of hypocritical pieties about "the right to life."

In this endless exchange of terrorist acts, each side claims it is "retaliating." We bombed Tripoli to retaliate for the discotheque. The discotheque may have been bombed to retaliate for our killing 35 Libyan seamen who were on a patrol boat in the Gulf of Sidra—in international waters, just as we were.

We were in the Gulf of Sidra supposedly to show Libya it must not engage in terrorism. And Libya says—indeed it is telling the truth in this instance—that the United States is an old hand at terrorism, having subsidized terrorist governments in Chile, Guatemala, and El Salvador, and right now subsidizing the terrorism of the contras against farmers, their wives, and children, in Nicaragua.

Does a Western democracy have more right to kill innocent people than does a Middle Eastern dictatorship? Even if we were a perfect democracy that would not give us such a license. But the most cherished element of our democracy—the pluralism of dissenting voices, the marketplace of contending ideas—seems to disappear at a time like this, when the bombs fall, the flag waves, and everyone scurries, as Ted Kennedy did, to fall meekly behind "our commander-in-chief." We waited for moral leadership. But Gary Hart, John Kerry, Michael Dukakis, and Tip O'Neill all muttered their support. No wonder the Democratic Party is in such pathetic shape.

Where in national politics are the emulators of those two courageous voices at the time of the Gulf of Tonkin incident in Vietnam—Wayne Morse and Ernest Gruening—who alone in the Senate refused to go along with "our commander-in-chief" in that first big military strike that launched the ten-year shame of Vietnam?

And where was our vaunted "free press"? After the bombing a beaming Shultz held a press conference for a group of obsequious reporters in Washington who buttered him up, who licked at his flanks, who didn't ask a single question about the morality of our action, about the civilians killed by our bombs in Tripoli. Where are the likes of I.F. Stone, who did in his little newsletter for so many years what no big American daily would do—raise hard questions? Why did Anthony Lewis and Tom Wicker, who sometimes raise such questions—melt away?

Terrorism now has two names, worldwide. One is Khadafi. One is Reagan. In fact, that is a gross simplification. If Khadafi were gone, if Reagan were gone, terrorism would continue—it is a very old weapon of fanatics, whether they operate from secret underground headquarters, or from ornate offices in the capitals of the superpowers.

Too bad Khadafi's infant daughter died, one columnist wrote. Too bad, he said, but that's the game of war. Well, if that's the game, then let's get the hell out of it, because it is poisoning us morally, and not solving any problem. It is only continuing and escalating the endless cycle of retaliation which will one day, if we don't kick our habits, kill us all.

Let us hope that, even if this generation, its politicians, its reporters, its flag-wavers and fanatics, cannot change its ways, the children of the next generation will know better, having observed our stupidity. Perhaps they will understand that the violence running wild in the world cannot be stopped by more violence, that someone must say: we refuse to retaliate, the cycle of terrorism stops here.

Columbus, the Indians, and Human Progress 1492-1992

The remarkable thing about 1992 was not the huge celebratory hoopla about the quincentennial of Christopher Columbus's voyage, but the fact that there was so much protest and opposition to that celebration. Hundreds and hundreds of meetings and activities around the country used the quincentennial to educate the American public about what Columbus did, and how that connects with our time. What we have here is a blending of two of my talks on the subject, at the University of Wisconsin and the University of Minnesota, accomplished by the daring publishers of the Open Magazine Pamphlet series. When Greg Bates asked me, "Do we need permission from them to reprint this?" I answered unhesitatingly, "No, these are unusual fellows, they *want* everybody in the world to reprint their stuff, no questions asked."

1992

George Orwell, who was a very wise man, wrote: "Who controls the past controls the future. And who controls the present controls the past." In other words, those who dominate our society are in a position to write our histories. And if they can do that, they can decide our futures. That is why the telling of the Columbus story is important.

Let me make a confession. I knew very little about Columbus until about twelve years ago, when I began writing my book *A People's History of the United States*. I had a Ph.D. in history from Columbia University—that is, I had the proper training of a historian, and what I knew about Columbus was pretty much what I had learned in elementary school.

But when I began to write my *People's History* I de-

cided I must learn about Columbus. I had already concluded that I did not want to write just another overview of
American history—I knew my point of view would be different. I was going to write about the United States from the
point of view of those people who had been largely neglected in the history books: the indigenous Americans, the
black slaves, the women, the working people, whether native or immigrant.

I wanted to tell the story of the nation's industrial
progress from the standpoint, not of Rockefeller and Carnegie and Vanderbilt, but of the people who worked in their
mines, their oil fields, who lost their limbs or their lives
building the railroads.

I wanted to tell the story of wars, not from the standpoint of generals and presidents, not from the standpoint of
those military heroes whose statues you see all over this
country, but through the eyes of the G.I.'s, or through the
eyes of "the enemy." Yes, why not look at the Mexican War,
that great military triumph of the United States, from the
viewpoint of the Mexicans?

And so, how must I tell the story of Columbus? I
concluded, I must see him through the eyes of the people
who were here when he arrived, the people he called "Indians" because he thought he was in Asia.

Well, they left no memoirs, no histories. Their culture
was an oral culture, not a written one. Besides, they had
been wiped out in a few decades after Columbus's arrival.
So I was compelled to turn to the next best thing: the
Spaniards who were on the scene at the time. First, Columbus himself. He had kept a journal.

His journal was revealing. He described the people
who greeted him when he landed in the Bahamas—they
were Arawak Indians, sometimes called Tainos—and told
how they waded out into the sea to greet him and his men,
who must have looked and sounded like people from another world, and brought them gifts of various kinds. He
described them as peaceable, gentle, and said: "They do not

bear arms, and do not know them for I showed them a sword—they took it by the edge and cut themselves."

Throughout his journal, over the next months, Columbus spoke of the native Americans with what seemed like admiring awe: "They are the best people in the world and above all the gentlest—without knowledge of what is evil—nor do they murder or steal...they loved their neighbors as themselves and they have the sweetest talk in the world...always laughing."

And in a letter he wrote to one of his Spanish patrons, Columbus said: "They are very simple and honest and exceedingly liberal with all they have, none of them refusing anything he may possess when he is asked for it. They exhibit great love toward all others in preference to themselves." But then, in the midst of all this, in his journal, Columbus writes: "They would make fine servants. With fifty men we could subjugate them all and make them do whatever we want."

Yes, this was how Columbus saw the Indians—not as hospitable hosts, but as "servants," to "do whatever we want."

And what did Columbus want? This is not hard to determine. In the first two weeks of journal entries, there is one word that recurs seventy-five times: **GOLD.**

In the standard accounts of Columbus, what is emphasized again and again is his religious feeling, his desire to convert the natives to Christianity, his reverence for the Bible. Yes, he was concerned about God. But more about Gold. Just one additional letter. His was a limited alphabet. Yes, all over the island of Hispaniola, where he, his brothers, his men, spent most of their time, he erected crosses. But also, all over the island, they built gallows—340 of them by the year 1500. Crosses and gallows—that deadly historic juxtaposition.

In his quest for gold, Columbus, seeing bits of gold among the Indians, concluded there were huge amounts of it. He ordered the natives to find a certain amount of gold within a certain period of time. And if they did not meet their quota, their arms were hacked off. The others were to learn from this and deliver the gold.

Samuel Eliot Morison, the Harvard historian who was Columbus's admiring biographer, acknowledged this. He wrote: "Whoever thought up this ghastly system, Columbus was responsible for it, as the only means of producing gold for export... Those who fled to the mountains were hunted with hounds, and of those who escaped, starvation and disease took toll, while thousands of the poor creatures in desperation took cassava poison to end their miseries."

Morison continues: "So the policy and acts of Columbus for which he alone was responsible began the depopulation of the terrestrial paradise that was Hispaniola in 1492. Of the original natives, estimated by a modern ethnologist at 300,000 in number, one-third were killed off between 1494 and 1496. By 1508, an enumeration showed only 60,000 alive...in 1548 Oviedo (Morison is referring to Fernandez de Oviedo, the official Spanish historian of the Conquest) doubted whether 500 Indians remained."

But Columbus could not obtain enough gold to send home to impress the King and Queen and his Spanish financiers, so he decided to send back to Spain another kind of loot: slaves. They rounded up about 1200 natives, selected 500, and these were sent, jammed together, on the voyage across the Atlantic. Two hundred died on the way, of cold, of sickness.

In Columbus's journal, an entry of September 1498 reads: "From here one might send, in the name of the Holy Trinity, as many slaves as could be sold..."

What the Spaniards did to the Indians is told in horrifying detail by Bartolome de las Casas, whose writings give the most thorough account of the Spanish-Indian encounter. Las Casas was a Dominican priest who came to the New World a few years after Columbus, spent forty years on Hispaniola and nearby islands, and became the leading advocate in Spain for the rights of the natives. Las Casas, in his book *The Devastation of the Indies,* writes of the Arawaks: "...of all the infinite universe of humanity, these people are the most guileless, the most devoid of wickedness and duplicity...yet into this sheepfold...there came some Spaniards who immediately behaved like ravening beasts...Their reason for killing and destroying...is that the Christians have an ultimate aim which is to acquire gold..."

The cruelties multiplied. Las Casas saw soldiers stabbing Indians for sport, dashing babies' heads on rocks. And when the Indians resisted, the Spaniards hunted them down, equipped for killing with horses, armor plate, lances, pikes, rifles, crossbows, and vicious dogs. Indians who took things belonging to the Spaniards—they were not accustomed to the concept of private ownership and gave freely of their own possessions—were beheaded, or burned at the stake.

Las Casas's testimony was corroborated by other eyewitnesses. A group of Dominican friars, addressing the Spanish monarchy in 1519, hoping for the Spanish government to intercede, told about unspeakable atrocities, children thrown to dogs to be devoured, new-born babies born to women prisoners flung into the jungle to die.

Forced labor in the mines and on the land led to much sickness and death. Many children died because their mothers, overworked and starved, had no milk for them. Las Casas, in Cuba, estimated that 7000 children died in *three months.*

The greatest toll was taken by sickness, because the Europeans brought with them diseases against which the natives had no immunity: typhoid, typhus, diphtheria, smallpox.

As in any military conquest, women came in for especially brutal treatment. One Italian nobleman named Cuneo recorded an early sexual encounter. The "Admiral" he refers to is Columbus, who, as part of his agreement with the Spanish monarchy, insisted he be made an Admiral. Cuneo wrote:

"...I captured a very beautiful Carib woman, whom the said Lord Admiral gave to me and with whom...I conceived desire to take pleasure. I wanted to put my desire into execution but she did not want it and treated me with her finger nails in such a manner that I wished I had never begun. But seeing that, I took a rope and thrashed her well...Finally we came to an agreement."

There is other evidence which adds up to a picture of widespread rape of native women. Samuel Eliot Morison wrote: "In the Bahamas, Cuba, and Hispaniola they found young and beautiful women, who everywhere were naked, in most places accessible, and presumably complaisant." Who presumes this? Morison, and so many others.

Morison saw the conquest as so many writers after him have done, as one of the great romantic adventures of world history. He seemed to get carried away by what appeared to him as a *masculine* conquest. He wrote:

"Never again may mortal men hope to recapture the amazement, the wonder, the delight of those October days in 1492, when the new world gracefully yielded her virginity to the conquering Castilians."

The language of Cuneo ("we came to an agreement"), and of Morison ("gracefully yielded") written almost five hundred years apart, surely suggests how persistent through modern history has been the mythology that rationalizes sexual brutality by seeing it as "complaisant."

So, I read Columbus's journal, I read Las Casas. I also read Koning's pioneering work of our time—*Columbus: His Enterprise*, which, at the time I wrote my *People's History*, was the only contemporary account I could find which departed from the standard treatment.

When my book appeared, I began to get letters from all over the country about it. Here was a book of 600 pages, starting with Columbus, ending with the 1970's, but most of the letters I got from readers were about one subject: Columbus. I could have interpreted this to mean that, since this was the very beginning of the book, that's all these people had read. But no, it seemed that the Columbus story was simply the part of my book that readers found most startling. Because every American, from elementary school on, learns the Columbus story, and learns it the same way: "In Fourteen Hundred and Ninety Two, Columbus Sailed the Ocean Blue."

How many of you have heard of Tigard, Oregon? Well, I hadn't, until, about seven years ago, I began receiving, every semester, a bunch of letters, twenty or thirty, from students at one high school in Tigard, Oregon. It seems their teacher was having them (knowing high schools, I almost said "forcing them") read my *People's History*. He was photocopying a number of chapters and giving them to the students. And then he had them write letters to me, with comments and questions. Roughly half of them thanked me for giving them data which they had never seen before. The others were angry, or wondered how I got such information, and how I had arrived at such outrageous conclusions.

One high school student named Bethany wrote: "Out of all the articles that I've read of yours I found 'Columbus, the Indians, and Human Progress' the most shocking." Another student named Brian, 17 years old, wrote: "An example of the confusion I feel after reading your article concerns Columbus coming to America…According to you, it seems he came for women, slaves, and gold. You say that Columbus physically abused the Indians that didn't help him find gold. You've said you have gained a lot of this information from Columbus's own journal. I am wondering if there is such a journal, and if so, why isn't it a part of our history. Why isn't any of what you say in my history book, or in history books people have access to each day."

I pondered this letter. It could be interpreted to mean that the writer was indignant that no other history books had told him what I did. Or, as was more likely, he was saying: "I don't believe a word of what you write! You made this up!"

I am not surprised at such reactions. It tells something about the claims of pluralism and diversity in American culture, the pride in our "free society," that generation after generation has learned exactly the same set of facts about Columbus, and finished their education with the same glaring omissions.

A school teacher in Portland, Oregon, named Bill Bigelow has undertaken a crusade to change the way the Columbus story is taught all over America. He tells of how he sometimes starts a new class. He goes over to a girl sitting in the front row, and takes her purse. She says: "You took my purse!" Bigelow responds: "No, I discovered it."

Bill Bigelow did a study of recent children's books on Columbus. He found them remarkably alike in their repetition of the traditional point of view. A typical 5th grade biography of Columbus begins: "There once was a boy who loved the salty sea." Well! I can imagine a children's biography of Attila the Hun beginning with the sentence: "There once was a boy who loved horses."

Another children's book in Bigelow's study, this time for second graders: "The king and queen looked at the gold and the Indians. They listened in wonder to Columbus's stories of adventure. Then they all went to church to pray and sing. Tears of joy filled Columbus's eyes."

I once spoke about Columbus to a workshop of school teachers, and one of them suggested that school children were too young to hear of the horrors recounted by Las Casas and others. Other teachers disagreed, said children's stories include plenty of violence, but the perpetrators are witches and monsters and "bad people," not national heroes who have holidays named after them.

Some of the teachers made suggestions on how the truth could be told in a way that would not frighten children unnecessarily, but that would avoid the falsification of history now taking place.

The arguments about children "not being ready to hear the truth" does not account for the fact that in American society, when the children grow up, they *still* are not told the truth. As I said earlier, right up through graduate school I was not presented with the information that would counter the myths told to me in the early grades. And it is clear that my experience is typical, judging from the shocked reactions to my book that I have received from readers of all ages.

If you look in an *adult* book, the *Columbia Encyclopedia* (my edition was put together in 1950 but all the relevant information was available then, including Morison's biography), there is a long entry on Columbus (about a thousand words) but you will find no mention of the atrocities committed by him and his men.

In the 1986 edition of the *Columbia History of the World*, there are several mentions of Columbus, but nothing about what he did to the natives. Several pages are devoted to "Spain and Portugal in America," in which the treatment of the native population is presented as a matter of controversy, among theologians at that time, and among historians today. You can get the flavor of this "balanced approach," containing a nugget of reality, from the following passage from that *History:*

> The determination of the Crown and the Church to Christianize the Indians, the need for labor to exploit the new lands, and the attempts of some Spaniards to protect the Indians resulted in a very remarkable complex of customs, laws, and institutions which even today leads historians to contradictory conclusions about Spanish rule in America...Academic disputes flourish on this debatable and in a sense insoluble question, but there is no doubt that cruelty, overwork and disease resulted in an appalling depopulation. There were, according to recent estimates, about 25 million Indians in Mexico in 1519, slightly more than 1 million in 1605.

Despite this scholarly language—"contradictory conclusions...academic disputes...insoluble question"—there is no real dispute about the facts of enslavement, forced labor, rape, murder, the taking of hostages, the ravages of diseases carried from Europe, and the wiping out of huge numbers of native people. The only dispute is over how much emphasis is to be placed on these facts, and how they carry over into the issues of our time.

For instance, Samuel Eliot Morison does spend some time detailing the treatment of the natives by Columbus and his men, and uses the word "genocide" to describe the overall effect of the "discovery." But he buries this in the midst of a long, admiring treatment of Columbus, and sums up his view in the concluding paragraph of his popular book *Christopher Columbus, Mariner,* as follows:

> He had his faults and his defects, but they were largely the defects of the qualities that made him great—his indomitable will, his superb faith in God and in his own mission as the Christ-bearer to lands beyond the seas, his stubborn persistence despite neglect, poverty and discouragement. But there was no flaw, no dark side to the most outstanding and essential of all his qualities—his seamanship.

Yes, his seamanship!

Let me make myself clear. I am not interested in either denouncing or exalting Columbus. It is too late for that. We are not writing a letter of recommendation for him to decide his qualifications for undertaking another voyage to another part of the universe. To me, the Columbus story is important for what it tells us about ourselves, about our time, about the decisions we have to make for our century, for the next century.

Why this great controversy today about Columbus and the celebration of the quincentennial? Why the indignation of native Americans and others about the glorification of that conqueror? Why the heated defense of Columbus by others? The intensity of the debate can only be because it is not about 1492, it is about 1992.

We can get a clue to this if we look back a hundred years to 1892, the year of the quadricentennial. There were great celebrations in Chicago and New York. In New York there were five days of parades, fireworks, military marches, naval pageants, a million visitors to the city, a memorial statue unveiled at a corner of Central Park, now to be known as Columbus Circle. A celebratory meeting took place at Carnegie Hall, addressed by Chauncey DePew.

You might not know the name of Chauncey DePew, unless you recently looked at Gustavus Myers's classic work, *History of the Great American Fortunes*. In that book, Chauncey DePew is described as the front man for Cornelius Vanderbilt and his New York Central railroad. DePew traveled to Albany, the capital of New York State, with satchels of money and free railroad passes for members of the New York State legislature, and came away with subsidies and land grants for the New York Central.

DePew saw the Columbus festivities as a celebration of wealth and prosperity—you might say, as a self-celebration. He said that the quadricentennial event "marks the wealth and civilization of a great people...it marks the things that belong to their comfort and their ease, their pleasure and their luxuries...and their power."

We might note that at the time he said this, there was much suffering among the working poor of America, huddled in city slums, their children sick and undernourished. The plight of people who worked on the land—which at this time was a considerable part of the population—was desperate, leading to the anger of the Farmers' Alliances and the rise of the People's (Populist) Party. And the following year, 1893, was a year of economic crisis and widespread misery.

DePew must have sensed, as he stood on the platform at Carnegie Hall, some murmurings of discontent at the smugness that accompanied the Columbus celebrations, for he said, "If there is anything I detest...it is that spirit of historical inquiry which doubts everything; that modern spirit which destroys all the illusions and all the heroes which have been the inspiration of patriotism through all the centuries."

So, to celebrate Columbus was to be patriotic. To doubt was to be unpatriotic. And what did "patriotism" mean to DePew? It meant the glorification of expansion and conquest—which Columbus represented, and which America represented. It was just six years after his speech that the United States, expelling Spain from Cuba, began its own long occupation (sporadically military, continuously political and economic) of Cuba, took Puerto Rico and Hawaii, and began its bloody war against the Filipinos to take over their country.

That "patriotism" which was tied to the celebration of Columbus, and the celebration of conquest, was reinforced in the Second World War by the emergence of the United States as the superpower, all the old European empires now in decline. At that time, Henry Luce, the powerful president-maker and multi-millionaire, owner of *Time, Life,* and *Fortune* (not just the publications, but the *things!*) wrote that the 20th Century was turning into the "American Century," in which the United States would have its way in the world.

George Bush, accepting the presidential nomination in 1988, said: "This has been called the American Century because in it we were the dominant force for good in the world...Now we are on the verge of a new century, and what country's name will it bear? I say it will be another American Century."

What arrogance! That the 21st century, when we should be getting away from the murderous jingoism of this century, should already be anticipated as an *American* century, or as any one nation's century. Bush must think of himself as a new Columbus, "discovering" and planting his nation's flag on new worlds because he called for a U.S. colony on the moon early in the next century. And forecast a mission to Mars in the year 2019.

The "patriotism" that Chauncey DePew invoked in celebrating Columbus was profoundly tied to the notion of the inferiority of the conquered peoples. Columbus's attack on the Indians was justified by their status as sub-humans. The taking of Texas and much of Mexico by the United States just before the Civil War was done with the same racist rationale. Sam Houston, the first governor of Texas, proclaimed: "The Anglo-Saxon race must pervade the whole southern extremity of this vast continent. The Mexicans are no better than the Indians and I see no reason why we should not take their land."

At the start of the 20th century, the violence of the new American expansionism into the Caribbean and the Pacific was accepted because we were dealing with lesser beings.

In the year 1900, Chauncey DePew, now a U.S. Senator, spoke again in Carnegie Hall, this time to support Theodore Roosevelt's candidacy for vice-president. Celebrating the conquest of the Philippines as a beginning of the American penetration of China and more, he proclaimed:

> The guns of Dewey in Manila Bay were heard across Asia and Africa, they echoed through the palace at Peking and brought to the Oriental mind a new and potent force among western nations. We, in common with the countries of Europe, are striving to enter the limitless markets of the east...These people respect nothing but power. I believe the Philippines will be enormous markets and sources of wealth.

Theodore Roosevelt, who appears endlessly on lists of our "great presidents," and whose face is one of the four colossal sculptures of American presidents (along with Washington, Jefferson, Lincoln) carved into Mount Rushmore in South Dakota, was the quintessential racist-imperialist. He was furious, back in 1893, when President Cleveland failed to annex Hawaii, telling the Naval War College it was "a crime against white civilization." In his book *The Strenuous Life*, Roosevelt wrote:

> Of course our whole national history has been one of expansion...that the barbarians recede or are conquered...is due

solely to the power of the mighty civilized races which have
not lost the fighting instinct.

An Army officer in the Philippines put it even more
bluntly:

> There is no use mincing words...We exterminated the
> American Indians and I guess most of us are proud of
> it...and we must have no scruples about exterminating this
> other race standing in the way of progress and enlighten-
> ment, if it is necessary...

The official historian of the Indies in the early 16th
century, Fernandez de Oviedo, did not deny what was done
to natives by the *conquistadores*. He described "innumerable
cruel deaths as countless as the stars." But this was acceptable, because "to use gunpowder against pagans is to offer
incense to the Lord."

(One is reminded of President McKinley's decision to
send the army and navy to take the Philippines, saying it
was the duty of the United States to "Christianize and civi-
lize" the Filipinos.)

Against Las Casas's pleas for mercy to the Indians, the
theologian Juan Gines de Sepulveda declared: "How can
we doubt that these people, so uncivilized, so barbaric, so
contaminated with so many sins and obscenities have been
justly conquered."

Sepulveda in the year 1531 visited his former college
in Spain and was outraged by seeing the students there
protesting Spain's war against Turkey. The students were
saying: "All war...is contrary to the Catholic religion."

This led him to write a philosophical defense of the
Spanish treatment of the Indians. He quoted Aristotle, who
wrote in his *Politics* that some people were "slaves by nature," who "should be hunted down like wild beasts in
order to bring them to the correct way of life."

Las Casas responded: "Let us send Aristotle packing,
for we have in our favor the command of Christ: Thou shalt

love thy neighbor as thyself."

The dehumanization of the "enemy" has been a necessary accompaniment to wars of conquest. It is easier to explain atrocities if they are committed against infidels, or people of an inferior race. Slavery and racial segregation in the United States, and European imperialism in Asia and Africa, were justified in this way.

The bombing of Vietnamese villages by the United States, the search-and-destroy missions, the My Lai massacre, were all made palatable to their perpetrators by the idea that the victims were not human. They were "gooks" or "Communists," and deserved what they received.

In the Gulf War, the dehumanization of the Iraqis consisted of not recognizing their existence. We were not bombing women, children, not bombing and shelling ordinary Iraqi young men in the act of flight and surrender. We were acting against a Hitler-like monster, Saddam Hussein, although the people we were killing were the Iraqi victims of this monster. When General Colin Powell was asked about Iraqi casualties he said that was "really not a matter I am terribly interested in."

The American people were led to accept the violence of the war in Iraq because the Iraqis were made invisible— because the United States only used "smart bombs." The major media ignored the enormous death toll in Iraq, ignored the report of the Harvard medical team that visited Iraq shortly after the war and found that tens of thousands of Iraqi children were dying because of the bombing of the water supply and the resultant epidemics of disease.

The celebrations of Columbus are declared to be celebrations not just of his maritime exploits but of "progress," of his arrival in the Bahamas as the beginning of that much-praised five hundred years of "Western civilization." But those concepts need to be re-examined. When Gandhi was once asked what he thought about Western civilization, he replied: "It would be a good idea."

The point is not to deny the benefits of "progress" and

"civilization"—by which is meant advances in technology, knowledge, science, health, education, and standards of living. But there is a question to be asked: progress yes, but at what human cost?

Is progress simply to be measured in the statistics of industrial and technological change, without regard to the consequences of that "progress" for human beings? Would we accept a Russian justification of Stalin's rule, including the enormous toll in human suffering, on the ground that he made Russia a great industrial power?

I recall that in my high school classes in American history when we came to the period after the Civil War, roughly the years between that war and World War I, it was looked on as the Gilded Age, the period of the great Industrial Revolution, when the United States became an economic giant. I remember how thrilled we were to learn of the dramatic growth of the steel and oil industries, of the building of the great fortunes, of the crisscrossing of the country by the railroads.

We were not told of the human cost of this great industrial progress: how the huge production of cotton came from the labor of black slaves, how the textile industry was built up by the labor of young girls who went into the mills at twelve and died at twenty-five; how the railroads were constructed by Irish and Chinese immigrants who were literally worked to death, in the heat of summer and cold of winter; how working people, immigrants and native-born, had to go out on strike and be beaten by police and jailed by National Guardsmen before they could win the eight-hour day; how the children of the working class in the slums of the city had to drink polluted water, and how they died early of malnutrition and disease. All this in the name of "progress."

And yes, there are huge benefits from industrialization, science, technology, medicine. But so far, in these five hundred years of Western civilization, of Western domination of the rest of the world, most of those benefits have gone to a small part of the human race. For billions of people in the Third World, they still face starvation, homelessness, disease, the early deaths of their children.

Did the Columbus expeditions mark the transition from savagery to civilization? What of the Indian civilizations which had been built up over thousands of years before Columbus came? Las Casas and others marveled at the spirit of sharing and generosity which marked the Indian societies, the communal buildings in which they lived, their aesthetic sensibilities, the egalitarianism among men and women.

The British colonists in North America were startled at the democracy of the Iroquois—the tribes who occupied much of New York and Pennsylvania. The American historian Gary Nash describes Iroquois culture: "No laws and ordinances, sheriffs and constables, judges and juries, or courts or jails—the apparatus of authority in European societies—were to be found in the northeast woodlands prior to European arrival. Yet boundaries of acceptable behavior were firmly set. Though priding themselves on the autonomous individual, the Iroquois maintained a strict sense of right and wrong..."

In the course of westward expansion, the new nation, the United States, stole the Indians' land, killed them when they resisted, destroyed their sources of food and shelter, pushed them into smaller and smaller sections of the country, went about the systematic destruction of Indian society. At the time of the Black Hawk War in the 1830's—one of hundreds of wars waged against the Indians of North America—Lewis Cass, the governor of the Michigan territory, referred to his taking of millions of acres from the Indians as "the progress of civilization." He said: "A barbarous people cannot live in contact with a civilized community."

We get a sense of how "barbarous" these Indians were when, in the 1880's, Congress prepared legislation to break up the communal lands in which Indians still live, into small private possessions, what today some people would call, admiringly, "privatization." Senator Henry Dawes, author of this legislation, visited the Cherokee Nation, and described what he found: "...there was not a family in that whole nation that had not a home of its own. There was not a pauper in that nation, and the nation did not owe a dollar...it built its own schools and its hospitals. Yet the defect of the system was apparent. They have got as far as they can go, because they own their land in common...there is not enterprise to make your home any better than that of your neighbors. There is no selfishness, which is at the bottom of civilization."

That selfishness at the bottom of "civilization" is connected with what drove Columbus on, and what is much-praised today, as American political leaders and the media speak about how the West will do a great favor to the Soviet Union and Eastern Europe by introducing "the profit motive."

Granted, there may be certain ways in which the incentive of profit may be helpful in economic development, but that incentive, in the history of the "free market" in the West, has had horrendous consequences. It led, throughout the centuries of "Western Civilization," to a ruthless imperialism.

In Joseph Conrad's novel *Heart of Darkness*, written in the 1890s, after some time spent in the Upper Congo of Africa, he describes the work done by black men in chains on behalf of white men who were interested in ivory. He writes: "The word 'ivory' rang in the air, was whispered, was sighed. You would think they were praying to it...To tear treasure out of the bowels of the land was their desire, with no more moral purpose at the back of it than there is in burglars breaking into a safe."

The uncontrolled drive for profit has led to enormous human suffering, exploitation, slavery, cruelty in the workplace, dangerous working conditions, child labor, the destruction of land and forests, the poisoning of the air we breathe, the water we drink, the food we eat.

In his 1933 autobiography, Chief Luther Standing Bear wrote:

> True the white man brought great change. But the varied fruits of his civilization, though highly colored and inviting, are sickening and deadening. And if it be the part of civilization to maim, rob, and thwart, then what is progress? I am going to venture that the man who sat on the ground in his tipi meditating on life and its meaning, accepting the kinship of all creatures, and acknowledging unity with the universe of things, was infusing into his being the true essence of civilization.

The present threats to the environment have caused a reconsideration, among scientists and other scholars, of the value of "progress" as it has been so far defined. In December of 1991 there was a two-day conference at MIT, in which fifty scientists and historians discussed the idea of progress in Western thought. Here is part of the report on that conference in the *Boston Globe*.

> In a world where resources are being squandered and the environment poisoned, participants in an M.I.T. conference said yesterday, it is time for people to start thinking in terms of sustainability and stability rather than growth and progress... Verbal fireworks and heated exchanges that sometimes grew into shouting matches punctuated the discussions among scholars of economics, religion, medicine, history and the sciences.

One of the participants, historian Leo Marx, said that working toward a more harmonious co-existence with nature is itself a kind of progress, but different from the traditional one in which people try to overpower nature.

So, to look back at Columbus in a critical way is to raise all these questions about progress, civilization, our relations with one another, our relationship to the natural world.

You probably have heard—as I have, quite often—that

it is wrong for us to treat the Columbus story the way we do. What they say is: "You are taking Columbus out of context, looking at him with the eyes of the 20th century. You must not superimpose the values of our time on events that took place 500 years ago. That is ahistorical."

I find this argument strange. Does it mean that cruelty, exploitation, greed, enslavement, violence against helpless people, are values peculiar to the 15th and 16th centuries? And that we in the 20th century are beyond that? Are there not certain human values which are common to the age of Columbus and to our own? Proof of that is that both in his time and in ours there were enslavers and exploiters; in both his time and ours there were those who protested against that, on behalf of human rights.

It is encouraging that, in this year of the quincentennial, there is a wave of protest, unprecedented in all the years of celebration of Columbus, all over the United States, and throughout the Americas. Much of this protest is being led by Indians, who are organizing conferences and meetings, who are engaging in acts of civil disobedience, who are trying to educate the American public about what really happened five hundred years ago, and what it tells us about the issues of our time.

There is a new generation of teachers in our schools, and many of them are insisting that the Columbus story be told from the point of view of the native Americans. In the fall of 1990 I was telephoned from Los Angeles by a talk-show host who wanted to discuss Columbus. Also on the line was a high school student in that city, named Blake Lindsey, who had insisted on addressing the Los Angeles City Council to oppose the traditional Columbus Day celebration. She told them of the genocide committed by the Spaniards against the Arawak Indians. The City Council did not respond.

Someone called in on that talk show, introducing herself as a woman who had emigrated from Haiti. She said: "The girl is right—we have no Indians left—in our last uprising against the government the people knocked down the statue of Columbus and now it is in the basement of the city hall in Port-au-Prince." The caller finished by saying: "Why don't we build statues for the aborigines?"

Despite the textbooks still in use, more teachers are questioning, more students are questioning. Bill Bigelow reports on the reactions of his students after he introduces them to reading material which contradicts the traditional histories. One student wrote: "In 1492, Columbus sailed the ocean blue... That story is about as complete as Swiss cheese."

Another wrote a critique of her American history textbook to the publisher, Allyn and Bacon, pointing to many important omissions in that text. She said: "I'll just pick one topic to keep it simple. How about Columbus?"

Another student: "It seemed to me as if the publishers had just printed up some glory story that was supposed to make us feel more patriotic about our country... They want us to look at our country as great and powerful and forever right... We're being fed lies."

When students discover that in the very first history they learn—the story of Columbus—they have not been told the whole truth, it leads to a healthy skepticism about all of their historical education. One of Bigelow's students, named Rebecca, wrote: "What does it matter who discovered America, really?... But the thought that I've been lied to all my life about this, and who knows what else, really makes me angry."

This new critical thinking in the schools and in the colleges seems to frighten those who have glorified what is called "Western Civilization." Reagan's Secretary of Education, William Bennett, in his 1984 "Report on the Humanities in Higher Education," writes of Western civilization as "our common culture...its highest ideas and aspirations."

One of the most ferocious defenders of Western civilization is philosopher Allan Bloom, who wrote *The Closing of the American Mind* in a spirit of panic at what the social

movements of the Sixties had done to change the educational atmosphere of American universities. He was fright-
ened by the student demonstrations he saw at Cornell,
which he saw as a terrible interference with education.

Bloom's idea of education was a small group of very
smart students, in an elite university, studying Plato and
Aristotle, and refusing to be disturbed in their contempla-
tion by the noise outside their windows of students rallying
against racism or protesting against the war in Vietnam.

As I read him, I was reminded of some of my colleagues, when I was teaching in a black college in Atlanta,
Georgia, at the time of the civil rights movement, who
shook their heads in disapproval when our students left
their classes to sit-in, to be arrested, in protest against racial
segregation. These students were neglecting their education, they said. In fact, these students were learning more in
a few weeks of participation in social struggle than they
could learn in a year of going to class.

What a narrow, stunted understanding of education!
It corresponds perfectly to the view of history which insists
that Western Civilization is the summit of human achieve-
ment. As Bloom wrote in his book: "...only in the Western
nations, i.e., those influenced by Greek philosophy, is there
some willingness to doubt the identification of the good
with one's own way."

Well, if this willingness to doubt is the hallmark of
Greek philosophy, then Bloom and his fellow idolizers of
Western civilization are ignorant of that philosophy.

If Western Civilization is considered the high point of
human progress, the United States is the best representative
of this civilization. Here is Allan Bloom again: "This is the
American moment in world history... America tells one
story: the unbroken, ineluctable progress of freedom and
equality. From its first settlers and its political foundings on,
there has been no dispute that freedom and equality are the
essence of justice for us..."

Yes, tell black people and native Americans and the

homeless and those without health insurance, and all the victims abroad of American foreign policy that America "tells one story...freedom and equality."

Western Civilization is complex. It represents many things, some decent, some horrifying. We would have to pause before celebrating it uncritically when we note that David Duke, the Louisiana Ku Klux Klan member and ex-Nazi says that people have got him wrong. "The common strain in my thinking," he told a reporter, "is my love for Western civilization."

We who insist on looking critically at the Columbus story, and indeed at everything in our traditional histories, are often accused of insisting on Political Correctness, to the detriment of free speech. I find this odd. It is the guardians of the old stories, the orthodox histories, who refuse to widen the spectrum of ideas, to take in new books, new approaches, new information, new views of history. They, who claim to believe in "free markets," do not believe in a free marketplace of ideas, any more than they believe in a free marketplace of goods and services. In both material goods and in ideas, they want the market dominated by those who have always held power and wealth. They worry that if new ideas enter the marketplace, that people may begin to rethink the social arrangements that have given us so much suffering, so much violence, so much war these last five hundred years of "civilization."

Of course we had all that before Columbus arrived in this hemisphere, but resources were puny, people were isolated from one another, and the possibilities were narrow. In recent centuries, however, the world has become amazingly small, our possibilities for creating a decent society have enormously magnified, and so the excuses for hunger, ignorance, violence, racism, no longer exist.

In rethinking our history, we are not just looking at the past, but at the present, and trying to look at it from the point of view of those who have been left out of the benefits of so-called civilization. It is a simple but profoundly important thing we are trying to accomplish, to look at the world from other points of view. We need to do that, as we come into the next century, if we want this coming century to be different, if we want it to be, not an American century, or a western century, or a white century, or a male century, or any nation's, any group's century, but a century for the human race.

"Je Ne Suis Pas un Marxiste"

I never expected to have a fancy title for a piece of mine. In fact, this essay appeared in Z *Magazine* under the title "Nothing Human is Alien to Me."

1988

Not long ago, someone referred to me publicly as a "Marxist professor." In fact, two people did. One was a spokesperson for "Accuracy in Academia," worried that there were "five thousand Marxist faculty members" in the United States (which diminished my importance, but also my loneliness). The other was a former student I encountered on a shuttle to New York, a fellow traveler. I felt a bit honored. A "Marxist" means a tough guy (making up for the pillowy connotation of "professor"), a person of formidable politics, someone not to be trifled with, someone who knows the difference between absolute and relative surplus value, and what is commodity fetishism, and refuses to buy it.

I was also a bit taken aback (a position which yoga practitioners understand well, and which is good for you about once a day). Did "Marxist" suggest that I kept a tiny statue of Lenin in my drawer and rubbed his head to discover what policy to follow to intensify the contradictions in the imperialist camp, or what songs to sing if we were sent away to such a camp?

Also, I remembered that famous statement of Marx: "Je ne suis pas un Marxiste." I always wondered why Marx, an English-speaking German who had studied Greek for his doctoral dissertation, would make such an important statement in French. But I am confident that he did make it, and I think I know what brought it on. After Marx and his wife Jenny had moved to London, where they lost three of their

145

six children to illness and lived in squalor for many years, they were often visited by a young German refugee named Pieper. This guy was a total "noodnik" (there are "noodniks" all along the political spectrum stationed ten feet apart, but there is a special Left Noodnik, hired by the police, to drive revolutionaries batty). Pieper (I swear, I did not make him up) hovered around Marx gasping with admiration, once offered to translate *Das Kapital* into English, which he could barely speak, and kept organizing Karl Marx Clubs, exasperating Marx more and more by insisting that every word Marx uttered was holy. And one day Marx caused Pieper to have a severe abdominal cramp when he said to him: "Thanks for inviting me to speak to your Karl Marx Club. But I can't. I'm not a Marxist."

That was a high point in Marx's life, and also a good starting point for considering Marx's ideas seriously without becoming a Pieper (or a Stalin, or a Kim Il Sung, or any born-again Marxist who argues that every word in Volumes One, Two, and Three of *Das Kapital*, and especially in the *Grundrisse*, is unquestionably true). Because it seems to me (risking that this may lead to my inclusion in the second part of Norman Podhoretz's *Register of Marxists, Living or Dead*), Marx had some very useful thoughts.

For instance, we find in Marx's short but powerful *Theses on Feuerbach* the idea that philosophers, who always considered their job was to interpret the world, should now set about changing it, in their writings, and in their lives.

Marx set a good example himself. While history has treated him as a sedentary scholar, spending all his time in the library of the British Museum, Marx was a tireless activist all his life. He was expelled from Germany, from Belgium, from France, was arrested and put on trial in Cologne.

Exiled to London, he kept his ties with revolutionary movements all over the world. The poverty-ridden flats that he and Jenny Marx and their children occupied became busy centers of political activity, gathering places for political refugees from the continent.

True, many of his writings were impossibly abstract (especially those on political economy; my poor head at the age of nineteen swam, or rather drowned, with ground rent and differential rent, the falling rate of profit and the organic composition of capital). But he departed from that constantly to confront the events of his time, to write about the revolutions of 1848, the Paris Commune, rebellion in India, the Civil War in the United States.

The manuscripts he wrote at the age of twenty-five while an exile in Paris, where he hung out in cafes with Engels, Proudhon, Bakunin, Heine, Stirner, often dismissed by hard-line fundamentalists as "immature," contain some of his most profound ideas. His critique of capitalism in those *Economic and Philosophic Manuscripts* did not need any mathematical proofs of "surplus value." It simply stated (but did not state it simply) that the capitalist system violates whatever it means to be human. The industrial system Marx saw developing in Europe not only robbed them of the product of their work, it estranged working people from their own creative possibilities, from one another as human beings, from the beauties of nature, from their own true selves. They lived out their lives not according to their own inner needs, but according to the necessities of survival.

This estrangement from self and others, this alienation from all that was human, could not be overcome by an intellectual effort, by something in the mind. What was needed was a fundamental, revolutionary change in society, to create the conditions—a short workday, a rational use of the earth's natural wealth and people's natural talents, a just distribution of the fruits of human labor, a new social consciousness—for the flowering of human potential, for a leap into freedom as it had never been experienced in history.

Marx understood how difficult it was to achieve this, because, no matter how "revolutionary" we are, the weight of tradition, habit, the accumulated mis-education of generations, "weighs like a nightmare on the brain of the living."

Marx understood politics. He saw that behind political conflicts were questions of class: who gets what. Behind benign bubbles of togetherness *(We* the people...*our* country...*national* security), the powerful and the wealthy would legislate on their own behalf. He noted (in *The Eighteenth Brumaire,* a biting, brilliant analysis of the Napoleonic seizure of power after the 1848 Revolution in France) how a modern constitution could proclaim absolute rights, which were then limited by marginal notes (he might have been predicting the tortured constructions of the First Amendment in our own Constitution), reflecting the reality of domination by one class over another regardless of the written word.

He saw religion, not just negatively as "the opium of the people," but positively as "the sigh of the oppressed creature, the heart of a heartless world, the soul of soulless conditions." This helps us understand the mass appeal of the religious charlatans of the television screen, as well as the work of Liberation Theology in joining the soulfulness of religion to the energy of revolutionary movements in miserably poor countries.

Marx was often wrong, often dogmatic, often a "Marxist." He was sometimes too accepting of imperial domination as "progressive," a way of bringing capitalism faster to the third world, and therefore hastening, he thought, the road to socialism. (But he staunchly supported the rebellions of the Irish, the Poles, the Indians, the Chinese, against colonial control.)

He was too insistent that the industrial working class must be the agent of revolution, and that this must happen first in the advanced capitalist countries. He was unnecessarily dense in his economic analyses (too much education in German universities, maybe) when his clear, simple insight into exploitation was enough: that no matter how valuable were the things workers produced, those who controlled the economy could pay them as little as they liked, and enrich themselves with the difference.

Personally, Marx was sometimes charming, generous, self-sacrificing; at other times arrogant, obnoxious, abusive. He loved his wife and children, and they clearly adored him, but he also may have fathered the son of their German housekeeper, Lenchen.

The anarchist Bakunin, his rival in the International Workingmen's Association, said of Marx: "I very much admired him for his knowledge and for his passionate and earnest devotion to the cause of the proletariat. But...our temperaments did not harmonize. He called me a sentimental idealist, and he was right. I called him vain, treacherous, and morose, and I was right."

Marx's daughter, Eleanor, on the other hand, called her father "the cheeriest, gayest soul that ever breathed, a man brimming over with humor..."

He epitomized his own warning, that people, however advanced in their thinking, were weighed down by the limitations of their time. Still, Marx gave us acute insights, inspiring visions. I can't imagine Marx being pleased with the "socialism" of the Soviet Union. He would have been a dissident in Moscow, I like to think. His idea of the "dictatorship of the proletariat" was the Paris Commune of 1871, where endless argument in the streets and halls of the city gave it the vitality of a grass-roots democracy, where overbearing officials could be immediately booted out of office by popular vote, where the wages of government leaders could not exceed that of ordinary workers, where the guillotine was destroyed as a symbol of capital punishment. Marx once wrote in the *New York Tribune* that he did not see how capital punishment could be justified "in a society glorying in its civilization."

Perhaps the most precious heritage of Marx's thought is his internationalism, his hostility to the national state, his insistence that ordinary people have no nation they must obey and give their lives for in war, that we are all linked to one another across the globe as human beings. This is not only a direct challenge to modern capitalist nationalism, with its ugly evocations of hatred for "the enemy" abroad, and its false creation of a common interest for all within certain artificial borders. It is also a rejection of the narrow nationalism of contemporary "Marxist" states, whether the Soviet Union, or China, or any of the others.

Marx had something important to say not only as a critic of capitalism, but as a warning to revolutionaries, who, he wrote in *The German Ideology*, had better revolutionize themselves if they intended to do that to society. He offered an antidote to the dogmatists, the hard-liners, the Piepers, the Stalins, the commissars, the "Marxists." He said: "Nothing human is alien to me."

That seems a good beginning for changing the world.

The Perils of Plato

For many years, in my course at Boston University, "Introduction to Political Theory," I used Plato's dialogues, *Apology* and *Crito*. It gave me some measure of respectability, since I was not giving an orthodox course in political theory; I was skipping back and forth from the Peloponnesian War to the Vietnam War, from Machiavelli to Kissinger. And in this case it enabled me to skip back and forth from Plato in the *Apology* (giving Socrates an inspiring speech on behalf of political courage) to Plato in the *Crito* (offering Socrates as a dutiful obeyer of the state that had wrongly sentenced him to death). When I.F. Stone's book on Socrates came out *(The Trial of Socrates)*, *Z Magazine* gave me this opportunity to comment on the state-worship of Plato, and to make fun of his great reputation as a master of the dialogue.

1988

I once heard I.F. Stone, queried about his extraordinary investigative reporting, say: "I'm having so much fun, I should be arrested." After reading his new book *The Trial of Socrates*, I am willing to testify against him. He is clearly having too much fun.

He is also (though classical scholarship seems far removed from journalism) carrying on the work he did in his famous *Weekly*. He has lowered himself (secretly, guilty of trespass) into the mine shaft, with his lamp, his pick and shovel, dug deep into the documents kept by the authorities, and emerged at the end of a long day with some brilliant nuggets, which he offers to the world, and which damn the authorities.

He shows us that the usefulness of history does not depend on its newness. Events of two thousand years ago can be as illuminating as those of yesterday; the ideas of people in ancient Athens are as familiar as those we read in the daily newspaper.

Stone, who once annoyed presidents and F.B.I. directors, is now irritating professional philosophers. He has moved into their territory, into the house they considered a private dwelling, indeed, into the best room, the one with Plato's *Complete Works*, in the original Greek. Lacking J. Edgar Hoover's resources, the philosophers are unable to let out a contract on I.F. Stone, except to book reviewers.

One of these, in the *New York Times*, said that Stone is "determinedly unsympathetic" (to Socrates, to Plato), full of "misconceptions," and had perhaps even "anti-intellectual prejudice."

For a long time Plato has been one of the untouchables of modern culture, his reputation that of an awesome mind, a brilliant writer of dialogue; his work the greatest of the Great Books. You don't criticize Plato without a risk of being called anti-intellectual.

I can't get excited, I confess, about the scholarly disputations in *The Trial of Socrates*. Like: should you trust Plutarch's or Diodorus Siculus's claim that the philosopher Anaxagoras was also the object of a political trial in Athens, when neither Thucydides nor Xenophon nor Plato mentioned it? Let I.F. Stone have his fun.

What is important is that Stone challenges the intellectual authorities of modern Western culture as brazenly as he has done with the political authorities.

It is easy for liberals and radicals to expose the Best and the Brightest as political advisers, like those Phi Beta Kissingers who gave Machiavellian advice to the warmakers of Vietnam. It seems harder to escape the thrall of the intellectual advisers, the Great Names and the Great Books. And even when we manage to do that, we may substitute our own, the Great Names and Great Books of the Left, thus replacing one cultural hegemony with another.

Surely we need more practice in challenging intellectual authority of all kinds. I.F. Stone sets a good example. And he picks the most formidable of targets, the great Plato.

If you have read Allan Bloom's book, *The Closing of the*

American Mind, you will notice that it was written in a state of shock and fear caused by the tumults of the 60s. There is no evidence of shock at the war in Vietnam, or at police dogs attacking blacks in Bull Connor's Birmingham, but there is hysteria over the fact that his Plato seminar was threatened with interruption by students demonstrating on the Cornell campus where he taught. In page after page, Bloom swoons over Plato.

He and his fellow conservatives have good reason to do so. And Western culture has good reason for making Plato a demigod, required reading for every educated person who will take his or her proper place in society. It is good to see that I.F. Stone, characteristically, refuses to be intimidated.

Socrates left no writings that we know of. (Maybe that's why he was executed. Publish or perish). So Plato put words in his mouth. This was shrewd, to *create* a character (we don't *really* know what Socrates was like) who could charm us, a wise, gentle man put to death by the government in Athens because he spoke his mind. The words coming from such a man will be especially persuasive.

But they are Plato's words, Plato's ideas. All we know of Socrates is what Plato tells us. Or what we read in recollections of another contemporary of his, Xenophon. Or what we can believe about him from reading his friend Aristophanes' spoof on Socrates in his play, *The Clouds.*

So we can't know for sure what Socrates really said to his friend Crito, who visited him in jail, after he had been condemned to death. But we do know that what Plato has him say, in the dialogue *Crito* (written many years after Socrates' execution in 399 B.C.), has been impressed, with or without attribution, on the minds of many generations, down to the present day, with deadly effect.

Plato's message is presented appealingly by a man calmly facing death. It is made even more appealing by the fact that it follows another dialogue, the *Apology*, in which Socrates addresses the jury in an eloquent defense of free speech, saying: "The unexamined life is not worth living."

Plato then unashamedly (lesson one in intellectual bullying: speak with utter confidence) presents us with some unexamined ideas. Having established Socrates' credentials as a martyr for independent thought, he proceeds in the *Crito* to put into Socrates' mouth an argument for blind obedience to government.

It is hardly a dialogue. Poor Crito is reduced to saying, to every one of Socrates' little speeches: "Yes...of course...clearly...I agree...Yes...I think that you are right...True..." And Socrates is going on and on, like the good trouper that he is, saying Plato's lines, making Plato's argument for him. We can't be sure these are Socrates' ideas. But we know they are Plato's because he makes an even more extended case for a totalitarian state in his famous *Republic*.

Crito offers to help Socrates escape from prison. Socrates replies: "No, I must obey the law. True, Athens has committed an injustice against me by ordering me to die for speaking my mind. But if I complained about this injustice, Athens could rightly say: 'We brought you into the world, we raised you, we educated you, we gave you and every other citizen a share of all the good things we could.'" Socrates accepts this, saying: "By not leaving Athens, I agreed to obey its laws. And so I will go to my death." (I'm paraphrasing, but not exaggerating.)

It is Plato's bumper-sticker: "Love it or leave it." Plato was the apostle of civil obedience. He did not live long enough to encounter the argument of Thoreau, who wrote a famous essay on civil disobedience. Thoreau said that whatever good things we have were not given us by the state, but by the energies and talents of the people of the country. And he would be damned if he would pay taxes to support a war against Mexico based on such a paltry argument.

Plato, the Western world's star intellectual, makes a number of paltry arguments in this so-called dialogue. He has the state say to Socrates (and Socrates accepts this so humbly one cannot believe this is the defiant orator of the *Apology*): "What complaint have you against us and the state, that you are trying to destroy us? Are we not, first of all, your parents? Through us your father took your mother and brought you into the world."

What complaint? Only that they are putting him to death! The state as parents? Now we understand those words: The Motherland, or The Fatherland, or The Founding Fathers, or Uncle Sam. It's not some little junta of military men and politicians who are sending you to die in some muddy field in Asia or Central America; it's your mother, your father, or your father's favorite brother. How can you say no?

Socrates listens meekly to the words of The Law: "Are you too wise to see your country is worthier, more to be revered, more sacred, and held in higher honor both by the gods and by all men of understanding, than your father and your mother and all your other ancestors; that you ought to reverence it and to submit to it...and to obey in silence if it orders you to endure flogging or imprisonment or if it send you to battle to be wounded or to die?"

Crito is virtually mute, a sad sack of a debater. You would think that Plato, just to maintain his reputation for good dialogue, would give Crito some better lines. But he took no chances. And so the admirable obligation one feels to one's neighbors, one's family, one's principles, indeed to other human beings wherever they reside on the planet, becomes confused with blind obedience to that disreputable artifice called government. And in that confusion, young men, going off to war in some part of the world they never heard of, for some cause that cannot be rationally explained, would say: "I owe it to my country."

These arguments are important, not because we want to make a judgment about Socrates or Plato or ancient Athens (it is too late for that), but because they are a way of thinking which every nation-state drums into the heads of its citizens from the time they are old enough to go to school. And because they show the perils of placing our trust, and the lives of our children, in the hands of the Experts, whether in politics or philosophy. It is not too late to try to overcome that.

And I was provoked to all of this by I.F. Stone, who was just having fun.

Failure to Quit

This essay (written for *Z Magazine* and updated for *Mobilizing Democracy: Changing the U.S. Role in the Middle East,* Common Courage Press, 1991) was inspired (if you are willing to call this an inspired piece) by my students of the Eighties. I was teaching a spring and fall lecture course with four hundred students in each course (and yet with lots of discussion). I looked hard, listened closely, but did not find the apathy, the conservatism, the disregard for the plight of others, that everybody (right and left) was reporting about "the me generation."

1990

I can understand pessimism, but I don't believe in it. It's not simply a matter of faith, but of historical evidence. Not overwhelming evidence, just enough to give hope, because for hope we don't need certainty, only possibility. Despite all those confident statements that "history shows..." and "history proves...," hope is all the past can offer us.

When I hear so often that there is little hope for change in the '90s, I think back to the despair that accompanied the onset of the '60s.

Historians of the late '40s and '50s (Richard Hofstadter, Louis Hartz) were writing ruefully about a liberal-conservative "consensus" that dominated the United States all through its history and that still prevailed, setting severe limits to change. Herbert Marcuse, at the start of the '60s, saw American society, American thought, as "one-dimensional," with radical ideas absorbed and deflected, dissent repressed through "tolerance."

One could not read these men, socially conscious, desirous themselves of change yet despairing of it, without feeling a deep pessimism about the possibilities for change in the United States. As the year 1960 began, Princeton philosopher Walter Kaufmann lamented the "uncommitted generation" and wrote: "What distinguishes them is that they are not committed to any cause." Neither he nor Hofstadter, Hartz, Marcuse, nor anyone for that matter, could have foreseen what would soon happen. It was unprecedented, unpredicted, and for at least fifteen years, uncontrollable. It would shake the country and startle the world, with consequences we are hardly aware of today.

True, those consequences did not include the end of war, exploitation, hunger, racism, military intervention, nationalism, sexism—only the end of legal racial segregation, the end of the war in Vietnam, the end of illegal abortions. It was just a beginning.

The age of apathy? I thought so too when, out of the Air Force, married, with two small children, finishing graduate work in history at Columbia University, I went south to teach in Atlanta, Georgia. My job was at Spelman College, where young black women, the daughters of railroad porters, teachers, ministers, maids, laborers, and farmers, came to get their degrees. It was 1956. The atmosphere on that tree-lined, fragrant campus was sedate, quiet, careful, and only close attention to what was said and left unsaid revealed deep resentment just below the surface. By 1960, these same quiet students were sitting in, demonstrating, picketing, going to jail. I learned that it was a serious mistake to interpret lack of action as lack of thought, lack of feeling. Rather, it was the absence of opportunities, openings, examples to emulate, groups to join—but when those appeared, the silence changed to uproar.

With the Gulf crisis there is a reaction that reaches beyond the student constituency into a much broader resistance to war. The Gulf crisis did not spring out of nowhere but rather was the product of many years of strife to which the United States contributed; so, too, it is clear that the activism that has risen against U.S. policies is the product of years of struggle. Resistance to war today is broadly based, and has significant new elements in it. The Military Families

Support Network is one example of this dynamic creativity. We are not out to shame the soldiers. We are helping them to resist.

Before the Gulf crisis there was much talk about the silence of the '80s. That silence deserves attention. In 1984 there was a silent majority in this country that refused to vote for Reagan: 68 percent of the eligible voters (add 21 percent who voted for Mondale with the 47 percent who didn't bother to vote). The unimpressive 32 percent who voted for Reagan was converted by a timid press and gullible public into an "overwhelming mandate." Four years later, in 1988, a majority of voters again refused to vote for Bush by similar margins.

But there is more than silence.

There is a human carry-over from the '60s. True, there are some veterans of those movements who have surrendered radical priorities for conventional "success." But there are others looking for openings and opportunities, pushing the system to its limits while pointing beyond, keeping the spirit of resistance alive. Many have been working steadily on various issues of peace and justice.

I think of my students at Spelman, among the many who were jailed during the Atlanta sit-ins: Marian Wright, going to Yale Law School, and to Mississippi with the Movement, now the tireless head of the Children's Defense Fund in Washington; Alice Walker, becoming a poet, a novelist, a feminist and political activist. I think of Carolyn Mugar, working with anti-war GIs in the Vietnam years, more recently a labor organizer in southern Massachusetts. Or Bernice Johnson Reagon, student leader and Freedom Singer in the Albany (Georgia) Movement of 1961-62, now a curator at the Smithsonian Institution, National Museum of American History, a formidable mind and voice, still a Freedom Singer (with Sweet Honey in the Rock). And Staughton Lynd, historian, organizer of Freedom Schools in Mississippi, anti-war protester of the '60s, now a labor lawyer in Ohio.

We all know such people, but it goes far beyond personal connections. There are thousands of local groups around the country—many more than existed in the '60s—devoted to struggling for tenants' rights or women's rights, or environmental protection, or against the arms race, or to take care of the hungry and homeless, or those in need of health care. There are now tens of thousands of professionals, many of them veterans of the movements of the '60s, who bring unorthodox ideas and humane values into courtrooms, classrooms, and hospitals.

Several years ago, when Reagan announced the blockade of Nicaragua, 550 of us sat in at the federal building in Boston to protest, and were arrested. It seemed too big a group of dissidents to deal with, and charges were dropped. The official complaint against all of us was: "Failure to Quit." That is, surely, the critical fact about the continuing movement for human rights here and all over the world.

Activism has worked. Over 50,000 people signed the Pledge of Resistance, committing themselves to protest against the U.S. intervention in Central America. A small number, but it represents a large part of the nation, because survey after survey has shown a majority of the country opposed to administration policy in Central America. True, the quick invasion of Panama met with little resistance. But is it not reasonable to assume that a U.S. invasion of Nicaragua, so lusted after by the Reagan Administration, was forestalled by recognition that the public would not support such an action? Congress, timid as it was, still had to respond to public opinion.

During the Iran-contra hearings, Oliver North chastised Congress repeatedly for not standing behind the president's policy in Nicaragua. Senator Patrick Leahy of Vermont, in exasperation, replied that Congress had no choice—mail was running so heavily against aid to the contras and invading Nicaragua that Congress didn't dare support Reagan's policy. Reagan's support for the contras was forced to become clandestine, and though enough havoc was created in Nicaragua to defeat the Sandinistas in the election, they have survived as an important force in the new situation.

When activists have committed civil disobedience to protest Central American policy, or the CIA, or the arms race, or U.S. actions in the Middle East, the degree of their support in the general public can be measured, at least roughly, by how juries of ordinary citizens react. During the war in Vietnam, when religious pacifists entered draft boards illegally to destroy draft records as a way of protesting the war, juries became increasingly reluctant to convict, and near the end of the war we saw the dramatic acquittal of the Camden 28 by a jury which then threw a party for the defendants.

Acts of civil disobedience during the '80s, at a much earlier stage of U.S. intervention than that in Vietnam, brought verdicts of acquittal whenever juries were permitted to listen to the defendants' reasons for their civil disobedience. In the spring of 1984, in Burlington, Vermont, the "Winooski 44" had occupied Senator Stafford's office to protest his support of aid to the contras. The jury, after hearing many hours of testimony about conditions in Nicaragua, the role of the CIA, and the nature of the contras, voted for acquittal. One of the jurors, a local house painter, said: "I was honored to be on that jury. I felt a part of history."

In Minneapolis that same year, seven "trespassers" protesting at the Honeywell Corporation were acquitted. In 1985, men and women blocked the Great Lakes Training Station in Illinois, others blocked the South African Embassy in Chicago, nineteen people in the state of Washington halted trains carrying warheads, and all these won acquittals in court. In western Massachusetts, where a protest against the CIA took place, there was another surprising acquittal. One of the jurors, Donna L. Moody, told a reporter: "All the expert testimony against the CIA was alarming. It was very educational."

Over the past six years, eighteen "Plowshares" actions, involving symbolic sabotage of nuclear weaponry, have resulted mostly in guilty verdicts. In the latest case, involving two Catholic priests and two others who broke into a naval air station near Philadelphia and damaged three aircraft, the judge refused the defense of "necessity" but allowed the jury to hear the defendants' reasons for their actions. The jury was unable to reach a verdict.

We hear many glib dismissals of today's college students and professionals as being totally preoccupied with money and self. There is obvious concern among students with their economic futures—evidence of the failure of the economic system to provide for the young, more than a sign of their indifference to social injustice. Still, the past few years have seen political actions on campuses all over the country. For 1986 alone, a partial list shows: 182 students calling for divestment from South Africa, arrested at the University of Texas; a black-tie dinner for alumni at Harvard called off after a protest on South African holdings; charges dropped against 49 Wellesley protesters after half the campus boycotted classes in support; and more protests recorded at Yale, Wisconsin, Louisville, San Jose, Columbia.

The activist message of "no more war," reflected in a divided public, has caused Bush to rush from one explanation to another in defending his Persian Gulf policy. In desperation, he keeps comparing Saddam Hussein to Hitler, trying to rekindle the popular support the government had in World War II. His outright promise in a press conference on December 4 that the Gulf crisis "would not be another Vietnam" is an acknowledgment of the deeply ingrained aversion to war that is a legacy of that terrible adventure.

But what about the others, the non-protesting students? Here, too, we must not underestimate the potential for change. Among the liberal arts students, business majors, and ROTC cadets in my classes, there have been superpatriots and enthusiasts of capitalism, but also others whose thoughts deserve some attention:

Writing in his class journal, one ROTC student, whose father was a navy flier, his brother a navy commander: "This one class made me go out and read up on South Africa. What I learned made me sick. My entire semester has been a paradox. I go to your class and I see a Vietnam vet named Joe Bangert tell of his experiences in the war. I was enthralled by his talk...By the end of that hour and a half, I hated the Vietnam War as much as he did. The only problem is that three hours after class I am marching around in my uniform—and feeling great about it. Is there something wrong with me? Am I being hypocritical? Sometimes I don't know..."

A young woman in ROTC: "What really stuck in my mind was the ignorance some people displayed at the end of class. We were discussing welfare. Some students stated that people on welfare were lazy, that if they really wanted to, they could find jobs. Argg! These rich kids (or middle class or whatever) who have all they need think they are so superior it makes me angry..."

The same student, after seeing the film *Hearts and Minds:* "General Westmoreland said 'Orientals don't value lives.' I was incredulous. And then they showed the little boy holding the picture of his father and he was crying and crying and crying... I must admit I started crying. What's worse was that I was wearing my Army uniform that day and I had to make a conscious effort not to disappear into my seat."

A young woman in the School of Management: "North broke the law, but will he be punished?...if he is let off the hook then all of America is punished. Every inner-city kid who is sent to jail for stealing food to feed his brothers and sisters is punished. Every elderly person who has to fight just to keep warm on a winter night will be punished...The law is supposed to be the common bond— the peace-making body. Yet it only serves the function se-

lectively—just when the people in control wish it to."
Surely history does not start anew with each decade.
The roots of one era branch and flower in subsequent eras.
Human beings, writings, invisible transmitters of all kinds,
carry messages across the generations. I try to be pessimis-
tic, to keep up with some of my friends. But I think back
over the decades, and look around. And then it seems to me
that the future is not certain, but it is possible.

About the Author

Howard Zinn is professor emeritus at Boston University. He is the author of the classic *A People's History of the United States*, "a brilliant and moving history of the American people from the point of view of those . . . whose plight has been largely omitted from most histories" *(Library Journal)*. Zinn has received the Lannan Foundation Literary Award for Nonfiction and the Eugene V. Debs award for his writing and political activism. He is the author of numerous books, including *The Zinn Reader*, the autobiographical *You Can't Be Neutral on a Moving Train*, and the plays *Marx in Soho* (South End Press) and *Emma* (South End Press).

Zinn grew up in Brooklyn and worked in the shipyards before serving as an Air Force bombardier in World War II. Zinn was chair of the History Department at Spelman College, where he actively participated in the civil rights movement, before taking a position at Boston University. He now lives with his wife, Roslyn, in Massachusetts and lectures widely on history and contemporary politics.

Seven of Zinn's books have been republished by South End Press as part of its new Radical Sixties series, which seeks to make available new editions of essential works that relate to or are inspired by the political struggles of the 1960s.

Books by Howard Zinn

Emma. Cambridge: South End Press, 2002.

Terrorism and War. New York: Seven Stories Press, 2002.

Howard Zinn on War. New York: Seven Stories Press, 2001.

Howard Zinn on History. New York: Seven Stories Press, 2001.

Marx in Soho: A Play on History. Cambridge: South End Press, 1999.

The Future of History: Interviews with David Barsamian. Monroe, Maine: Common Courage Press, 1999.

A People's History of the United States: 1492–Present, Twentieth Anniversary Edition. New York: HarperCollins, 1999.

The Zinn Reader: Writings on Disobedience and Democracy. New York: Seven Stories Press, 1997.

You Can't Be Neutral on a Moving Train: A Personal History of Our Times. Boston: Beacon Press, 1994.

Declarations of Independence: Cross-Examining American Ideology. New York: HarperCollins, 1990.

The Politics of History, 2nd ed. Urbana: University of Illinois Press, 1990.

See also the other six volumes by Howard Zinn in the South End Press Radical Sixties series.

The Radical Sixties Series

Failure to Quit is volume 7 in South End Press's new Radical Sixties series, which seeks to make available new editions of essential works that relate to or are inspired by the political struggles of the 1960s. Other titles in the series are:

Volume 1
SNCC: The New Abolitionists
by Howard Zinn
ISBN 0-89608-679-8
$15.00

Volume 2
The Southern Mystique
by Howard Zinn
ISBN 0-89608-680-1
$15.00

Volume 3
Vietnam: The Logic of Withdrawal
by Howard Zinn
ISBN 0-89608-681-X
$15.00

Volume 4
Disobedience and Democracy: Nine Fallacies of Law and Order
by Howard Zinn
ISBN 0-89608-675-5
$15.00

Volume 5
Postwar America: 1945–1971
by Howard Zinn
ISBN 0-89608-678-X
$15.00

Volume 6
Justice in Everyday Life: The Way It Really Works
by Howard Zinn
ISBN 0-89608-677-1
$15.00

Volume 8
Prelude to Revolution: France in May 1968
Second Edition
by Daniel Singer
ISBN 0-89608-676-3
$15.00

About South End Press

South End Press is a nonprofit, collectively run book publisher with more than 200 titles in print. Since our founding in 1977, we have tried to meet the needs of readers who are exploring, or are already committed to, the politics of radical social change.

Our goal is to publish books that encourage critical thinking and constructive action on the key political, cultural, social, economic, and ecological issues shaping life in the United States and in the world. In this way, we hope to give expression to a wide diversity of democratic social movements and to provide an alternative to the products of corporate publishing.

To order books, please send a check or money order to: South End Press, 7 Brookline Street, #1, Cambridge, MA 02139-4146. Or call 1-800-533-8478. Please include $3.50 for postage and handling for the first book and 50 cents for each additional book. Write or e-mail us at southend@southendpress.org for a free catalog, or visit our website at http://www.southendpress.org.